GYPSIES IN SOCIAL SPACE

BY DIANA DENHAM

PALO ALTO, CALIFORNIA

Published By

RAGUSAN PRESS
936 Industrial Avenue
Palo Alto, California 94303

Adam S. Eterovich
Publisher

Library of Congress Catalog Card Number
80-51689

I.S.B.N.
0-918660-14-9

Copyright 1981
by
Diana Denham

TABLE OF CONTENTS

TABLE OF CONTENTS iii

LIST OF TABLES v

LIST OF FIGURES vii

LIST OF MAPS ix

ACKNOWLEDGEMENTS xi

Chapter

I	INTRODUCTION	1
II	HISTORICAL REVIEW	6
	Linguistic Evidence	7
	Physiological Evidence	8
	Origin	10
	Early Migration	10
	European Development	13
	American Development	19
	World Distribution	20
III	RESISTANCE TO ASSIMILATION	31
	Cultural System	31
	Boundary Maintaining Mechanisms	32
	Inflexible Internal Structure	37
	Self-Correcting Mechanisms	41
	Nature of the Contact Situation	44
	Conjunctive Relations	47
	Cultural Processes Activated	49
	Incorporation	49
	Replacement	50
	Fusion	50
	Isolation	50
	Summary	51
IV	SOCIAL AND CULTURAL PROCESSES CREATING SPATIAL PATTERNS AND BEHAVIORS	52
	Territoriality	56
	Communication	60
	Mobility	65
	Inter-City Migration	65
	Intra-City Change in Residence	66

	Inter-Regional Circulation	67
	Consumership	68
	Summary	70
V	SEATTLE ROM	72
	History	72
	Resistance to Assimilation	73
	Cultural System	73
	Contact Situation and Conjunctive Relations	76
	Assimilation Processes Activated	80
	Social and Cultural Processes Which Create Spatial Patterns and Behaviors	81
	Cultural Demands	97
	Social Demands	98
	Economic Demands	99
	Special Consumer Demands	99
VI	CONCLUSION	101
	BIBLIOGRAPHY	105

LIST OF TABLES

Table		Page
1	Dates of Gypsy Appearance in Europe	15
2	Gypsy Population in Eastern Europe (1970 estimates)	23
3	Gypsy Population in Western Europe (1970 estimates)	25
4	Gypsy Population in North and South America	27
5	Age Cohort Distributions for Seattle Gypsies and Seattle Gadjo	82
6	Sex Ratio for the Seattle Gypsy Population Compared with the Seattle Population	86
7	Gypsy Household Size and Number of Children in 32 Family Sample	89
8	Fiscal Budget 1976-77 - Gypsy Alternative School	94

LIST OF FIGURES

Figure		Page
1	Hierarchy of Gypsy Associations	34
2	Examples of Gypsy Patrin (sign language)	40
3	Generalized Diagram of Constraints on Individual Freedom	53
4	Romani Cultural System	55
5	Seattle Gypsy Fortune Telling Advertisements	79
6	Percentage of Total Populations by Age Cohort	83
7	Sex Ratios for Seattle Gypsy and Gadjo Populations	88

LIST OF MAPS

Map		Page
1	Gypsy Migrations in Asia	12
2	Gypsy Migrations in Europe	14
3	Concentrations of the Gypsy Populations in the United States	29
4	Residential Location of Gypsy Households in Seattle, Northend Sample	91
5	Census Tract Locations of Gypsy Households in Seattle, Northend Sample	92

ACKNOWLEDGEMENTS

To Joseph Velikonja

CHAPTER 1

INTRODUCTION

The urban environment nurtures many diverse lifestyles which often represent the degree of affluence attained by the various social groups in the population. Within the complex society of any metropolitan area a number of small social groups are often easily identified and, in general, they occupy a lower social position than the more dominant groups in the population. Some groups, such as criminals, prostitutes or skid road residents, are perceived by most people as undesirable, though existentially tolerated as members of the urban complex. These pariah groups frequently are constrained to a particular area of urban space. However, non-members may freely move in and out of the same space. Consequently, the group exercises less real control over their own social and spatial environment than do the majority of other urban dwellers. These groups "exist" on the urban social fringe and at the expense and often the mercy of those segments of the general population with which they come into direct contact.

This somewhat uncertain type of existence occurs in yet another group, but because they have greater spatial control over their activities, they likewise have control of their social environment. Although they too live in the nebulous urban social fringe, the members are much more hidden from the casual observer because they are spatially integrated with the total population. Nevertheless, they remain outside the social institutions utilized by the majority of the population. This group, variously termed "Hidden Americans" (Sutherland, 1975), "Urban Nomads" (Gropper, 1967), and the "Secret People" (Webb, 1960) are known to most people simply as "Gypsies". All of these designations are appropriate for a group of people who can be found in most large cities, and who refer to themselves as "Rom".[1] The manner, motivation and consequences of maintaining their social and cultural isolation, while achieving spatial integration within the urban complex are the subjects of this research.

During the search for information about the Rom, it became quite obvious that there were a great number of contradictions and inconsistencies in the available descriptive literature. This situation was also very apparent in the contemporary attitudes of both Gypsies and Gadjos (non-Gypsies). Understandably, as with any social group, there are differences between the ideal goals and practical reality. Perhaps, because of the unique lifestyle, the differences seem to be more highly magnified in the Gypsy culture and can be more easily observed.

For example, among the higher aspirations of Gypsies are those articulated by authors such as Ian Hancock and Grattan Puxon, both supporters of a world Romani movement. Hancock calls for the establishment of a geographical state called "Romanestan"; a country with international representation, organized and managed by descendants of today's Rom, and without Gadjo interference (Hancock, 1975, p. 54). Puxon is a bit more subdued, when in a recent letter (Oct. 8, 1975) he discusses the 2nd World Romani Congress which was held the first week in March, 1976 in Chandigarh, India:

> The purpose of the Congress is to gain Indian recognition for the Romani people, which in turn will back up our claim for nationality status in East Europe. Nationality status in turn will give us the formal right to form Romani organizations (where they do not already exist), to use the Romani language in schools, to publish Romani newspapers and to have regular broadcasts in Romanes on radio and tv. . . .
>
> This would usher in a renaissence which in turn, we believe, would be reflected in the smaller Romani communities in Western Europe and in America. If we can promote a sense of 'competition' between the host governments of communist East Europe, the USA and anywhere else in how much each is doing for their Gypsies (?) then we will be succeeding.
>
> Providing, and its an if to be watched carefully, any government assistance programmes include decision-making by Rom and are not aimed simply at assimilation. Hence again the 'nationality status' is important to ward off piece-meal assimilation.

In contrast to the high aspirations of the two authors, the Gypsies living in places like Seattle, Portland, New York, etc. hold much less ambitious objectives. These Gypsies, 95% of whom are illiterate, seem more concerned with the daily effort to survive. Their income is uncertain; much of their time is spent in acquiring everyday necessities. Most have no desire for a country of their own, nor do they in fact have any knowledge of people such as Hancock and Puxon. The gap between the realities of everyday life and the ideal goals seems to be too great to be bridged in the near future.

A contradiction also exists between the views of non-

Gypsies. Very few scholarly works by contemporary writers can be considered reliable in their presentation of the complex structure of Gypsy culture. Most Americans have very little, if any, interaction with Gypsies. It is doubtful if they would recognize a Gypsy. Consequently, most people have limited or incorrect information regarding the group. The concept of "Gypsy" (wanderer; stereotypic image) is nevertheless very much a part of American culture. Yet rarely, if ever, is there an association between the concept of "Gypsy" and the present day members of a thriving community found in our urban centers. Again, the chasm between the make believe and the real is very wide.

In the pages which follow, relevant information from the literature about Gypsies is combined with the findings collected from field work with local Gypsy families.[2] The Rom as a group have successfully resisted assimilation through the centuries. The causes and consequences of their isolation are found in social, cultural and spatial parameters. Before examining these parameters more closely it will be useful to review, first, just who the Rom are, and secondly, how their culture developed over time. Then it will be possible to see how the past and present behaviors have fostered the social and cultural isolation of the Rom, and enabled them to resist complete assimilation. By examining behavior of contemporary Rom it is possible to uncover spatial patterns which have evolved from these cultural and social processes. Their special social and cultural behaviors illustrate a unique example of urban spatial dynamics.

FOOTNOTES--CHAPTER I

[1] Throughout this paper the two terms, "Rom" and "Gypsy" will be used synonymously. In general, Rom is used among the Romani people, while Gypsy is used by non-Rom.

[2] Because of the precarious position of the financial support for many of the Gypsy programs in Seattle, it was essential that while pursuing my research objectives I make no impact on the Gypsy community or in any way interfere with their activities. Therefore, I was unable to function as a participant observer. The problem was partially overcome with the help of Ms. Cemeno, who has established good rapport with the Seattle Rom community, and who actved as my liaison.

CHAPTER 2

HISTORICAL REVIEW

It will be helpful if the term "Gypsy" is defined. Among gypsiologists there is a continuing debate regarding who should be called true Gypsies. However, the Gypsies themselves do not seem to have this difficulty. Over the years many different criteria have been utilized by Gadjo[1] to define a Gypsy. It has even been proposed that the term be used to include all traveling people or nomadic populations (Puxon; p. 3). Some scholars suggest that only people of Romany origins or with Romany "blood" be classified as Gypsies. Still others feel the "best criterion" is the knowledge of some dialect of Romanes (Gypsy language) (Sutherland, p. 14). Three possible reasons to account for the uncertainty are intermarriage, the term "Gypsy" and the secrecy of the Rom. The intermarriage of Gypsies with Gadjo, which even though small in number, still provides for some mixing with the non-Gypsy groups. Secondly, the word "Gypsy" has connotations which today are very different from the original meaning.[2] The word conveys an image rather than a reality. There are many people traveling today whose lifestyle resembles that of the Gypsy. Since the Gypsy will often keep his activities private, these other travelers are often mistaken as Rom.

In this study we will use the term "Gypsy" for people who have both Romany origins and speak Romanes. They call themselves Rom and believe themselves to be of true Romany blood.

What then are the Romany origins? Early in the nineteenth century gypsiologists began to investigate seriously evidence that the ancestors of the European Gypsies originated on the Indian sub-continent. Most of the early evidence on Gypsy origins was based solely on linguistics. In 1972 strongly supportive evidence, using finger dermatoglypics, added credence to the theory of Indian origin. Likewise in 1973 research involving factor investigation of various blood types and characteristics reinforced earlier findings. Thus, the evidence which is available today supports the theory that the origin of the European Gypsies, and subsequently the American Rom is in the north western corner of the Indian sub-continent.

Linguistic Evidence

The language of the Gypsies is called Romani, Romanes or Romany. It is an unwritten language, though it has been recorded and published by several non-Gypsies and neo-Gypsy scholars (Lee; p. 58). The most noteworthy study of the language was done by John Sampson in 1926. He devised a phonetic alphabet to record the speech of the Welsh Gypsies. However, his work is unfortunately of little value for contemporary usage because of the changes in the language over time. There are continuing efforts today by the National Gypsy Education Council in England to record the language and teach reading and writing of Romanes through correspondence courses (Roma, Vol. I).

More than half of the "fundamental vocabulary" of Romanes is related to dialects and/or groups of languages still spoken in northern India today (Clébert, p. 235). Romanes is among a group of dialects derived from a now non-existent mother tongue. Others in the group are Hindi, Cashmiri and Gujarati. The basic vocabulary of Romanes is quite close to that of Hindi and much of the grammar and lexicon can be explained only by Sanskrit (Clébert, p. 235).

The Romanes as used today is not a pure Indian dialect. Even though its origin has been traced unquestionably to northern India, it has been substantially modified through time as the Gypsies, with their language, moved over the globe. Words and phrases were accepted into their speech with each sojourn in a foreign land. The degree of incorporation of new words perhaps depended on the length of time spent at each new location (Clébert, p. 236). The process of language modification continued through many generations of traveling Gypsies and is still in operation today. This successive language variation over time has allowed linguists to trace the pattern of spatial movement which the Gypsies have followed over the centuries. Thus, not only do we know the approximate point of origin, but we also can map the general pathways of their moves using linguistic evidence.

Physiological Evidence

Two more recent investigations lend supportive evidence regarding the question of Gypsy origin. The first is a study by Stanislaw Marcinkiewicz published in 1972. In his study 300 Polish Gypsies were examined using "dermatoglyphic finger patterns" (Marcinkiewicz, p. 309). Analysis was made using

"Czekanowski's method of mean differences" in finger prints. Comparisons with other European population groups and other Gypsy groups permitted the author to draw several conclusions.

> 1. The connections found between the Polish gypsies and Hindu populations as regards dactyloscopic features point to the continuity of biological isolation of the majority of European gypsies lasting since their migration from the native geographical territories nine centuries ago...
> 2. The genetical value of dermatoglyphics is supported also by the lack of statistically significant differences in dermatoglyphics between various gypsy groups whereas such differences are found as between gypsies and other European populations.
> 3. The connections in dermatoglyphic features found between the Polish gypsies and Parsees and Khasi and Rajput castes present a possibility of a more accurate explanation of ethnogenesis...
> (Marcinkiewicz, p. 334)

Marcinkiewicz clearly places Polish and other European Gypsies among people who have northern Indian ancestry. Perhaps more importantly, his work gives proof of the historical social isolation of the Rom which persists to the present day. This aspect will be further examined in later chapters.

Another attempt to trace Gypsy origins was published in 1973. The research, conducted by Rex-Kiss, Szabo, Szabo and Hartmann, used the investigation of various blood types and characteristics. The Gypsy population of Hungary was the subject of the work.

> Comparison of the authors results with those of blood and serum group examinations performed on Indian (Pakistani) populations show that the phenotype and gene frequency values of Hungarian Gypsies are similar to those of North-and especially North West Indian (Pakistani) populations. On that basis the authors consider their results as evidence of North Indian origin of European Gypsies. (Rex-Kiss, Szabo', Szabo', Hartmann, p. 61)

Origin

The evidence cited here from linguistics and physiology support the belief, held by most investigators, that Northwest India is the general area of European Gypsy origin. The connections between the basic Gypsy language and the dialects of northern India have led Clébert to hypothesize that "tribes of authentic Gypsies" (Clébert, p. 45) are still living in India. They are yet to be identified, located and enumerated in the census of India to support his theory. It seems feasible that some original Gypsies (Rom) stayed in India and did not join the more nomadic migrants many centuries ago. Changes at the origin and modifications occurring over this long period of migration would make the two groups dissimilar today.

Early Migration

Since Romanes is not a written language, no documents have ever been preserved by the Gypsies themselves. Historical investigation of the early Gypsy migrations have been reconstructed by Clébert and others using not only linguistic evidence but also various historical documents, travelers accounts and indirect references to the "Gypsy-like" people (Clébert, p. 51). Much of the data in the historical reports are from very scattered sources and are often contradictory. Consequently such data should be used with caution. The dates and causes for the early Gypsy migrations from India are not known. However, most gypsiologists do speculate on both questions.

The consensus is that the pre-Gypsy tribes of northern India had been subjected to numerous invasions from the north.

Clébert suggests that the "Gypsies formed a fairly loose conglomerate of nomad tribes, dispersed over northern India" (Clébert, p. 5). With the arrival of the Aryans in 1500 B.C. the northern reaches of India suffered frequent onslaught of attack by Persians, Scythians, Kusheans, Greeks and later the Huns and Mussulmans (Moslems) (Clébert, p. 51). With each new encroachment the Rom were persecuted and usurped of their possessions. Thus, migration was probably a major instrument in the resolution of social, political and economic problems in their homeland.

The date of the "Tragic spectacle of the dispersal of a people" as Clébert so dramatically refers to it, is most often set by gypsiologists at between 855 and 1000 A.D. The routes followed by the Gypsies are presumed to be those used since classical times by other travelers. Leaving northern India, Gypsy bands traveled northwest through present day Pakistan and into Afghanistan across the Khyber Pass. Movement continued westward probably following more than one route, yet progressing along the lines of least resistance. No mention is made in the literature as to the size of the migrant population, and indeed there is no way to ascertain the number of participants. In Persia they separated into groups. One group headed northerly along the southern shore of the Caspian Sea. They made their way into Armenia and to the Caucasus mountains. Much later this group spread into southern Russia (Map No. 1).

A second major group continued along the northern end of the Persian Gulf and through Mesopotamia along the Tigris and Euphrates Rivers. At the headwaters the larger southern group

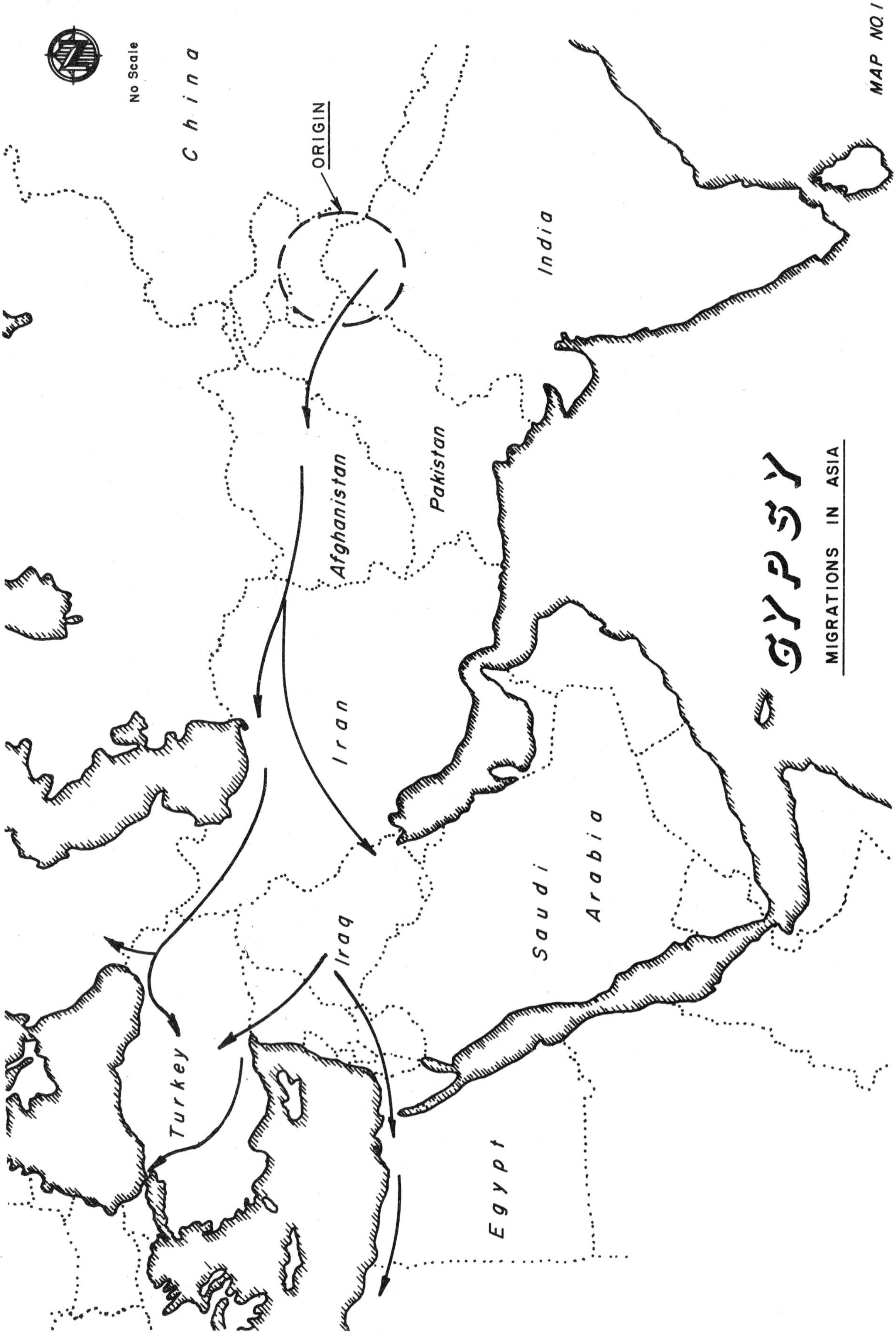

GYPSY
MIGRATIONS IN ASIA
MAP NO. 1
No Scale
ORIGIN
China
India
Pakistan
Afghanistan
Iran
Iraq
Saudi
Arabia
Turkey
Egypt

split again. Some of the tribes made their way to the Black Sea, while a second group reached the eastern Mediterranean and continued southward into Egypt. Eventually this second group traversed North Africa and crossed into Spain over the Strait of Gibralter (Clébert, p. 50).

The main body of emigrants spent a lengthy sojourn in the interior of Asia Minor before crossing into Greece and the Balkans.

By the end of the fourteenth century the Gypsies had reached the Balkan Peninsula and within the following century, in a second major wave of dispersion, the Gypsies spread throughout Europe (Map No. 2).

The dates of the Gypsies appearance in various European countries has been documented in archival records and are generally accepted as reliable. The dates represent the acknowledgement of the presence of Gypsies, usually by the official government authorities, though this does not preclude the presence of Gypsies at an earlier date. Shown in Table 1 are the probable dates of appearance in various regions and countries of Europe.

It is necessary to remember we have covered five centuries of migrations, fifteen or more generations of Gypsies. During these years there were changes not only linguistically but also in genetics. Despite their isolated existence from the majority populations, it would be unrealistic to presume there was no intermixing with the local populations in various regions.

European Development

The reaction in Europe to the presence of the Gypsies

GYPSY
MIGRATIONS THROUGH EUROPE

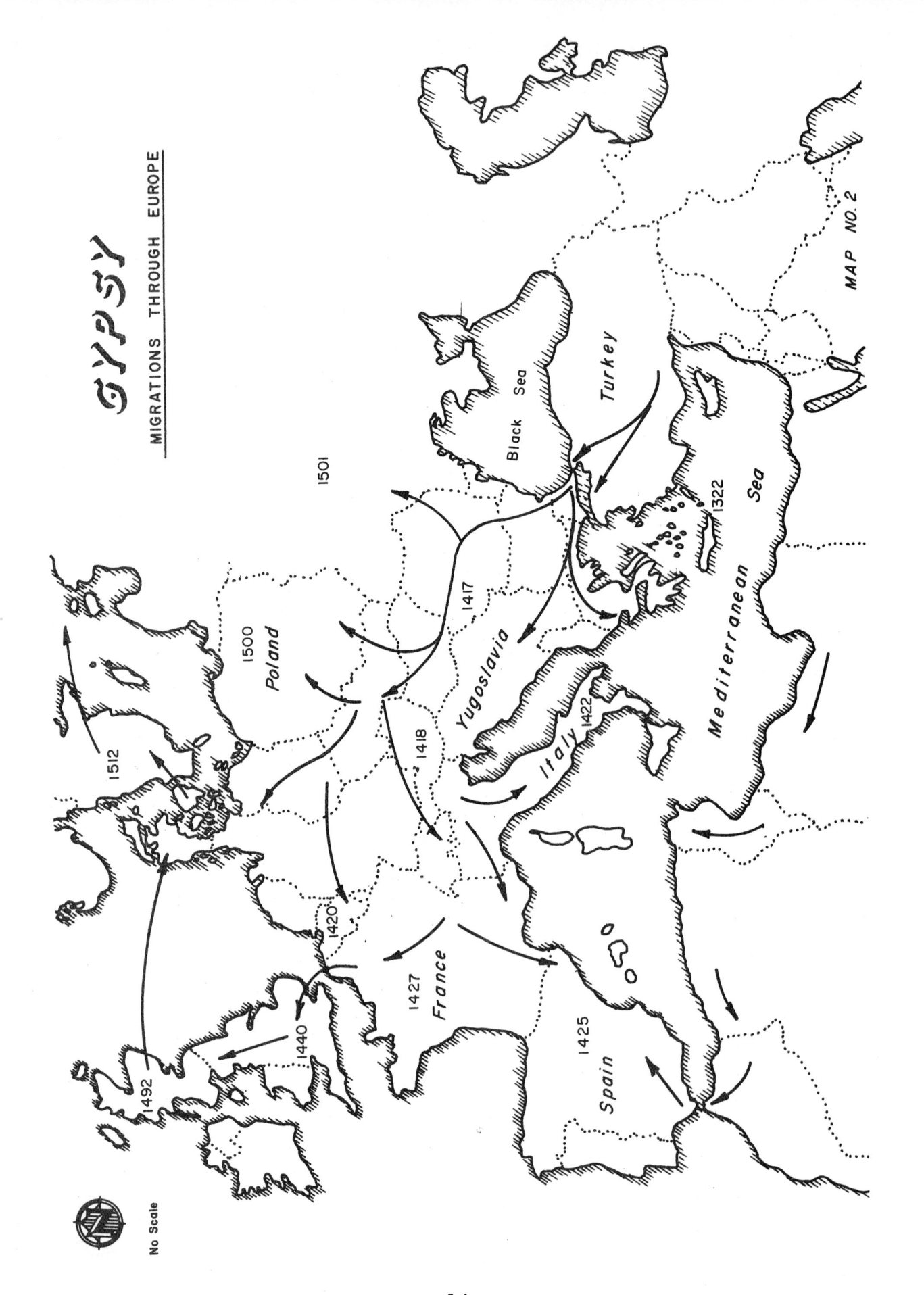

MAP NO. 2

TABLE 1

DATES OF GYPSY APPEARANCE IN EUROPE

1260 or 1399 A.D.	Bohemia
1322	Crete
1346	Corfu
1348	Serbia
1370	Wallachia
1378	Zagreb
1378	The Peloponnese
1414	Basle
1416 or 1417	Transylvania
1416 or 1417	Moldavia
1416 or 1417	The Elbe
1417	Central Europe (Germany)
1418	Saxony
1418	Augsburg
1418	Switzerland
1419	France
1419	Sisteron
15th Century	Belorussia
1420	Belgium
1420	Denmark
1422	Bologna
1422	Rome
1427	Paris
1430 or 1440	Wales
1425 or 1447	Barcelona
1492 or 1505	Scotland
1500 or 1501	Russia
1500 or 1509	Poland
1512 or 1515	Sweden
1512	Finland (from Sweden)
1514 or 1531	England
16th Century	Lithuania
16th or 17th Century	Ukraine
18th Century	Moscow

Source: Clébert, p. 54-55; McDowell, p. 16-17; Tokarev, p. 906.

gives us insight into the influences on the development of the Gypsy culture. Most of the societies responded to the Gypsies in a similar manner, differing only by degree and method. At first, these strangers were met with curiosity and interest and were given sanctions to travel freely. Later, their lifestyle was seen as incompatible with respectable society, and they were banished in most countries. This was followed by open persecutions and harassments. In order to defend themselves against the host societies, the Gypsies created for themselves a social and cultural environment of their own, totally divorced from the Gadjo social institutions. Their forced and self-imposed nomadic lifestyle reinforced their isolation and their own perception of the world.

Numerous accounts of the persecutions of the Gypsies in Europe begin about 1447. Before that time it appears that Gypsies were given safe conduct for various reasons. Some Gypsies carried letters issued by sovereigns of the areas in which they traveled. Many traveling people of this period carried similar letters of recommendation, some genuine, some fake. The certificates carried by the Gypsies stated that the bearer must atone for his past sins by vagabondage and subsistence by alms (Clébert, p. 58).[3] The most common story states the Gypsies claimed to be Egyptians who had been "commanded by God to embark on a seven-year period of wandering as penance" for one of a variety of reasons.[4] Many Gypsies using similar stories supposedly obtained these letters of safe conduct and accordingly were received favorably in Christian cities by nobility, clergy and other local dignitaries. This was probably one of the first and most well documented confidence games ever perpetuated by the Gypsies. Throughout history, whether consciously or by accident, the Gypsies learned how to manipulate the Gadjo world for their own benefits. They capitalized on the uniqueness of their appearance and culture. They began to deal in occupations which many of the local populations had learned to mistrust, such as horse-dealing, exhibition of performing animals, smiths, hawkers, fortune tellers and "Quack consultants about everything--all of them liable to excommunication" (Clébert, p. 79). As time passed these occupations came to be associated with the Gypsies in most parts of Europe.

From the end of the fifteenth century the Gypsies had been considered part of the so-called "dangerous class". This was the beginning of their persecution. One report describes Gypsies in the following statement:

> Gypsies. . . lead a vagabond existence everywhere on earth, they camp outside towns, in the fields and at crossroads, and there set up their huts and tents, depending for a living on highway robbery, stealing, deceiving and barter, amusing people with fortune-telling, purporting to tell the future by palmistry and other impostures. . .[5]

No one knows how or when the Gypsies developed fortune-telling, but it has become the most well known and widely practiced of their occupations. It continues today as a major source of income for many Gypsies.

The first official acts of repression in France were issued in Paris in 1539. The parliament of Paris records an expulsion order against the Gypsies, and in 1560 the States General of Orleans decreed that all "imposers known as Egyptians or Bohemians should leave the kingdom under penalty of the ships galley" (Clébert, p. 87-88).

In Germany they were first accepted as religious crusaders but were soon put into a "category of diabolical creatures" (Clébert, p. 106) associated with plagues and epidemics of all sorts. In their role as culture carriers they, more than likely, did on occasion carry more than culture between localities. At any rate, Gypsies were declared outlaws, and the native inhabitants were given the legalized right to shoot them on sight (Clébert, p. 106).

In Hungary and the area of present day Romania the Gypsies were accused of "heinous" crimes such as abduction of children, rape and even cannibalism. In order to exemplify the punishment to Gypsies, the authorities sought the most spectacular methods of punishment. These included hanging, beheading, or other public dismembering (Clébert, p. 102).

In both Russia and the Scandinavian countries, there seems to have been little if any repressive acts or real resistence to the Gypsies, according to Clébert.

There were early attempts to banish the Gypsies from Poland in the 16th century. However by the end of the 18th century there was more clemancy toward them, and they were allowed to reside peacefully until early in the 20th century (Clébert, p. 108).

In the British Isles the most severe repressions occurred in 1563 when Queen Elizabeth I accused the Gypsies of hiding religious emissaries and priests from Rome. Under penalty of death they were ordered to leave the country (Clébert, p. 111).

The process was similar in Spain in the latter 15th and early 16th centuries; first sanctions, then banishment, followed by real persecutions.

All of these attempts at ridding Europe of its Gypsies failed. In the 19th century and the early part of the 20th century many countries initiated programs directed at assimilation of the Gypsies, but these also failed. The Gypsies have remained a semi-nomadic social isolate to the present day.

These early European experiences of the Gypsies forged the social and cultural bonds which would sustain their particular way of life. By turning inward and rejecting the outside world theirs became a self-perpetuating system which renewed itself with each new generation. Traditions and social norms were established and rigidly maintained by the group. The behavior of both the Gypsies and the Gadjo to each other in European history is probably the single most important element in the preservation of the Gypsies as a distinct ethnic group.

American Development

At the turn of the century the complexion of Europe was changing rapidly; political unrest and hostilities between countries were increasing. Many Gypsies began to seek better places to live and to escape from Gadjo conflicts of which they were not a part (Yoors, 1967, p. 239). This was a time of major immigration to the United States and Canada. That is not to say that Gypsies were not present on the American continents long before 1900. There are several early reports of Gypsies being exiled to American and Brazilian colonies by Spain, Portugal, France and England which may indeed be true, but there is no real proof. It is reasonable to assume that there were various groups of Gypsies in this country before the major influx between 1880 and 1924. The principal stock of the present day Rom in the United States is most likely of Eastern European ancestry.

The life of the Gypsy in the United States was much the same as it had been in Europe. Traveling in small groups, living in tents or wagons, criss-crossing the country, yet meeting in large groups for annual events, for weddings or for funerals.

Evidence of Gypsy travelers in the Northwest is found as early as 1903. In November of that year a lengthy article appeared in *The Coast* magazine published in Seattle. The article by Honor L. Wilhelm attempted to alleviate misunderstandings about the Gypsies by explaining elements of their lifestyle. Wilhelm shows the Gypsies in a rather liberal and insightful manner, which seems incongruous for the time. The article also contains photographs including "a typical gypsy camp near Seattle" (*The Coast*, p. 156).

As America grew, industrialized and urbanized, the Gypsies gave up the horses and wagons for cars and trailers. They still continued to travel as before, until the depression of the 1930's. Much of their mobility was ended by gas and other types of rationing during this period. They were forced by necessity to spend more of their time in urban areas, and this marked the beginnings of their conversion from rural to urban nomads.

World Distribution

Prejudice and persecution have followed the Rom into the Twentieth Century, reaching horrifying heights in the World War II years. Over a quarter of a million Gypsies were deliberately eliminated during the war. In spite of these adversities the Rom hold to their traditions and social organization, which provides them with a measure of stability. Today their population is increasing by one quarter million per year according to Puxon (Puxon, 1973, p. 8), or 3% per year for an estimated total of 8 million.

Political boundaries drawn in Europe after World War II severely constrained migratory populations. The political institutions which accompanied these more rigid boundaries also exerted pressures on the Romani population which was still mobile to settle down. Contrary to popular Gadjo belief, in most countries the majority of Rom are either completely settled or semi-settled. Even the most nomadic Rom generally follow a set pattern of circulation, often spending the winter and/or the summer at the same locations. Puxon contends that only one third of the Romani population is still nomadic. However, even the most sedentary Gypsies in the United States change residence much more frequently than their Gadjo neighbors. A great deal of traveling is done during the summer months to visit friends, and relatives, or to attend festivities. Thus, in most countries which have Gypsies, there are two Romani populations: the traveling Rom[6] and the settled Rom.

The total number of Rom in the world today is estimated at between six (Hancock, 1974, p. 36) and eight and a half million (Puxon, June 6, 1974, correspondence). These estimates are not generally based on collected census data. No country in the world provides comprehensive statistics on the Rom. The two most obvious reasons for poor data collection are definition and registration.

Even Sweden, which is held in high esteem by demographers as the superior collector of population statistics falls short when enumerating the Rom. Sweden, like most other countries, has a problem with definition. Rom are counted with a portion of the population known as "travelers" and designated as "Tartar". These travelers include a group of people ". . . often characterized by an itinerant mode of living and by certain occupations" (Heymowski, p. 97). This group includes many non-Gypsies; people with mixed ancestry part of which may be Gypsy; and the pure Gypsies. As Heymowski's research suggests, ". . . of all those who appear in official sources only a few are recorded in a way which makes it possible to determine whether they are genuine Gypsies or not (Heymowski, p. 95).

The same type of problem exists in Great Britain and Ireland where traveling people may be classified as Gypsies, when in reality they are half-Gypsies (Didikois), mumpers (no Romani blood), or tinkers (itinerant workers in tin). Distinctions between these categories are often dubious. In France various nomadic groups and social isolates, such as the "cogots" are presumed to be included in the statistics (Heymowski, p. 95).

In the United States, both immigration and census data are collected without reference to ethnic or cultural origin of the population. Rom in the United States, when enumerated in the census, are reported as "white".

The second major problem, which is perhaps more significant, deals with the process of registration. Puxon states that Gypsies in Eastern Europe prefer to register under categories other than Gypsy in order to avoid the prejudicial treatment usually directed at Rom. By doing so, the aggregate statistics are made invalid. In the United States, the census forms are either ignored by the Rom or completed improperly with regard to race.

In some countries only the traveling Rom are enumerated, while in others, only the settled population is included in the census. There are also countries in which they are ignored completely (Puxon, p. 6).

It is necessary that we use the estimates of population as a general guide to the relative size of the Gypsy population and not as an enumeration of the world's Rom. There are three important areas of Romani concentration today: Eastern Europe, Western Europe, and the Americas. In no country do they represent a majority, and indeed in all countries where significant numbers are present they constitute only a small percentage of the total population. Tables 2, 3 and 4 present Puxon's population estimates of Rom in some of the countries with relatively large numbers. The tables are followed by a brief summary and generalizations about the position of Rom today in each of these areas.

TABLE 2

GYPSY POPULATION IN EASTERN EUROPE
(1970 estimates)

Yugoslavia	650,000
Romania	540,000
Hungary	480,000
U.S.S.R.	414,000
Bulgaria	363,000
Czechoslovakia	300,000
Poland	52,000
Albania]	50,000
TOTAL	2,849,000

Source: Puxon, p. 5-8.

Almost three million Rom now live in communist/socialist Eastern Europe. Since World War II these countries have had programs designed for the assimilation of the Gypsy populations. The degree of success varies greatly. Most of the programs made no allowances for the cultural bias or traditions of the Rom. Rather the governments simply prohibited the nomadic way of life and assumed integration would then be inevitable. This type of logic did produce sedentary Gypsies, but not assimilated Gypsies.

Poland, Czechoslovakia and the U.S.S.R. have laws against nomadism, while Romania has laws against horse-dealing and requires school attendance by the Rom. The laws and government provisions for housing and employment have all but ended the "traveling life" in Eastern Europe. Only two countries, Romania and Yugoslavia, still have many Rom on the roads.

In Eastern Europe today the Romani population exists in two divergent classes. The first is an educated "intelligentsia" which is seeking recognition of the Rom as a distinct national minority group with their "own schools and state-sponsored cultural associations" (Puxon, p. 7). The second, and larger group can be characterized by illiteracy, unemployment, shanty-town houses and inadequate health care. Many Rom in Eastern Europe have been settled for generations and have succeeded in Gadjo jobs. Some are engineers, secretaries, and physicians according to McDowell (McDowell, 1970, p. 121), but most are employed in the more traditional occupations of the Rom, such as in handicrafts and various repairs, and as unskilled labor rather than as professionals.

The situation in Western Europe is a bit more grim for

TABLE 3

GYPSY POPULATION IN WESTERN EUROPE
(1970 estimates)

Spain	500,000
France	190,000
Italy	80,000
West Germany	70,000
Britain	50,000
Greece	45,000
Portugal	40,000
Netherlands	30,000
Belgium	14,000
Ireland	10,000
Switzerland	10,000
Austria	9,000
Sweden	8,000
Finland	6,000
Norway	4,000
Denmark	3,000
TOTAL	1,069,000

Source: Puxon, p. 5-8.

Gypsies. The majority of Rom in this area are mobile. Political boundaries are often very rigid and restrictions on their movements are usually present. Most are illiterate and live near the poverty level.

In France they must carry a "caret de circulation" identifying them as Gypsies and as travelers. Caravan dwellers must register their children in schools at each stop, yet the Rom of France are still 90% illiterate (Puxon, p. 9). France also has a large number of semi-sedentary Rom. Many of them, along with Romani migrant laborers, mainly from Yugoslavia, and Spanish emigrants, live temporarily in the notorious bidonvilles of Marseilles, Paris and other large urban areas.

In Belgium the situation is similar but less severe. They

must carry a special "carte de nomade" to be presented on demand. Rom are no longer admitted to Belgium and caravans may reside at one place for a maximum of 24 hours. Puxon states that the Rom are allowed to occupy camps for longer periods at the more undesirable locations such as "municipal refuse tips" [fringe of garbage dumps] (Puxon, p. 10). In spite of the higher rate of infant mortality, disease and discomfort experienced at the more unhealthy locations, the Rom find them useful in providing some privacy. Some Gypsies in Europe deal in scrap materials such as metal and iron, in this case the refuse dumps often provide them with materials which they can sell.

The Netherlands has led the way in providing caravan sites with community buildings to help meet the educational and social needs for the Rom. Many Rom now spend the entire year on these municipal caravan sites (Puxon, p. 11).

In Britain the 1968 Caravan Sites Act states that "local authorities must provide sites for Gypsies 'residing or resorting to' their area". Gypsies are often fined for failing to camp on the official sites, and the local authorities have had difficulty establishing accommodations in all areas (Ministry of Housing and Local Government, 1967). A research team in 1974 "concluded that the achievements of the 1968 Act had been rather limited" (Sibley, p. 23).

Sibley has suggested "the need for further research on the demographic characteristics, migrations, economic activity and social networks of travelers" in order to make new legislation more responsive to the needs of the traveling population (Sibley, 1975, p. 24). The National Gypsy Council has severely criticized the 1968 Act for its inadequacies, yet it stands as the most comprehensive effort of any country to aid the Gypsy population.

The Scandinavian countries have fewer Rom than most other European countries. Sweden has a generally higher standard of living than its neighbors, and thus many Rom seek entry into Sweden but only a small number are admitted each year, according to Puxon.

The situation in West Germany is much like that of France but on a smaller scale. Semi-settled Rom occupy camps, small ghettoes or the less desirable areas of the cities, while migrant Rom from Yugoslavia, Turkey and Spain add to the already underhoused and underemployed ranks of foreign workers (A.B.C., 1975).

TABLE 4

GYPSY POPULATION IN NORTH AND SOUTH AMERICA
(1970 estimates)

United States	50,000 to 1,500,000
Canada	50,000
Brazil	15,000
Mexico	10,000
Argentina	10,000
TOTAL	1,585,000

Source: Puxon, p. 5-8.

Population estimates for the United States are less reliable than for most of the European countries. Cohn estimates around "20,000 Rom in North America" (Cohn, p. 23), while Hancock estimates one to two million Rom in the United States alone (Hancock, p. 36).

The truth probably falls somewhere in between these two extremes and more closely approximates the estimate given in the *Seattle Times* (June, 1975) of 250,000. It is impossible to determine which number is correct.

Compared to the European countries, the United States and Canada have been the places of greatest freedom for the Rom. The sheer size of both countries has allowed the Rom to move great distances without restrictions by the governments. This coupled with the higher standard of living in North America has allowed the Rom to successfully adapt their way of living to attain a much more economically comfortable existence than their counterparts elsewhere.

The Rom in North America have become an almost completely urban population. Map No. 3 locates 65 major urban areas of Gypsy concentrations in the United States.[7] There are no estimates of the population size in these areas and several areas of known concentration have been omitted by Gropper. No comprehensive research has been done on the Rom in North America; the few studies which have been done are on selected groups in specific areas.

FOOTNOTES--CHAPTER II

[1]Gadjo is the Romanes word meaning non-Gypsy. It may be spelled numerous ways depending on the source of reference. It also has gender and number, both of which I omit for simplicity.

[2]Gypsy is actually a contraction of the word Egyptian, and was applied to a specific group of people.

SEE FOOTNOTE & TEXT, p.28

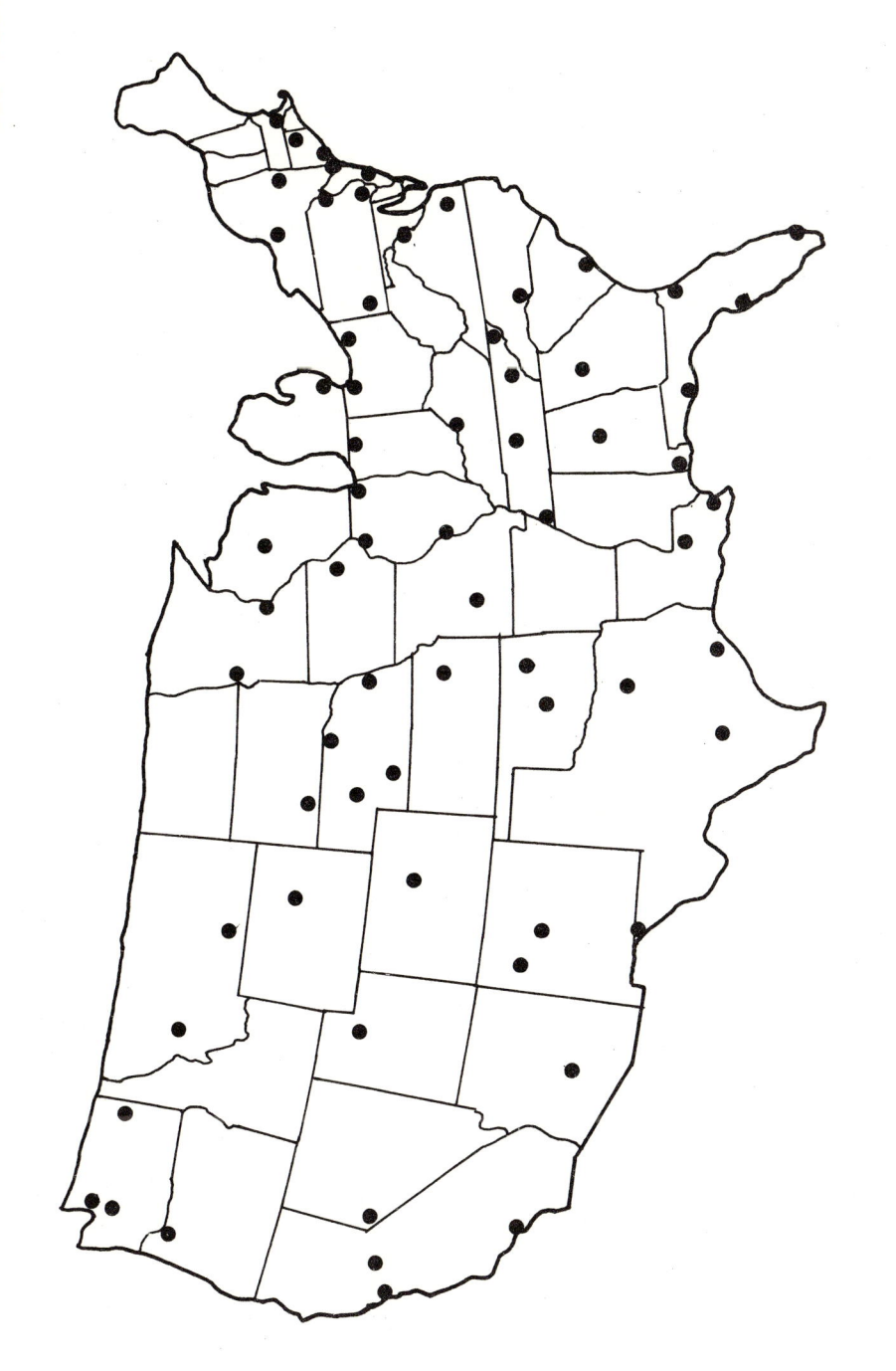

CONCENTRATIONS OF THE GYPSY POPULATIONS IN THE UNITED STATES - GROPPER, 1975

Map 3

[3] Other categories of wandering persons using "Letters of Protection" were the Golliards, the Coquillarts, the Rubins and the Convertis. A bibliography on this subject was compiled by Vexliard in 1956 entitled, *Introduction à la Sociologie du Vagabondage*.

[4] Several books relate the story of the exile in some detail. Some of the more interesting accounts are by Clébert, Liegeois and in specific volumes of *Etudes Tsiganes*.

[5] "Agrippa of Netteisheim, a German philosopher, medical doctor and alchemist who led a lively existence and associated with Gypsies..." quoted in Clébert, p. 77, from *Paradoxes sur l' incertitude des sciences*.

[6] Seattle Rom refer to these Gypsies as "fly-by-nights" which they sometimes do.

[7] Map No. 3 is adapted from Gropper, p. 19, and is intended for general reference only.

CHAPTER 3

RESISTANCE TO ASSIMILATION

Throughout history the Rom have resisted attempts at integration with the non-Gypsy population. They have retained a distinct sub-culture. The Rom are what Redfield (Redfield, 1947, p. 297) defines as a folk society; a small, non-literate, isolated and homogeneous group with a strong sense of solidarity. Today the Rom are no longer a spatially isolated population. However they have been able to remain culturally separated from the dominant society. They have survived, and indeed thrived, as a social community and have repeatedly, with success, adjusted to new environments.

How have the Rom accomplished the aforementioned, i.e. using the artifacts of other cultures or making accommodative changes, yet not being completely assimilated, or losing their cultural identity? In this context, it would be useful to reflect on four basic elements: (1) the Gypsy culture itself, (2) the nature of the contacts with other cultures, (3) the conjunctive relations between the Gypsy and non-Gypsy cultures, and (4) the cultural processes activated by the conjunction of the systems (Bee, 1974, p. 96).

I. Cultural System

The maintenance of a cultural system is based on an identity system. The Gypsy culture has three important characteristics: Boundary maintaining mechanisms which limit participation to a well defined in-group; Inflexible internal structures; and Self-correcting mechanisms which act to balance conflict and cohesion (Bee, 1974, p. 98). These three properties exist in many cultures which have remained independent despite infringement by outside influences. They are present in the culture complex of the Gypsies.

A. Boundary Maintaining Mechanisms

Boundaries can be maintained by a number of methods, in general any activity or ideology which controls ingress and interaction with aliens. This boundary enforcement can be thought of as a means of producing a closed system from which outsiders are carefully and continuously excluded. Many of the boundary controlling methods are subtle rather than deliberate. In essance, any activity or ideology which strengthens the group's ethnocentrism (i.e., conviction that somehow the members are better than members of other cultures) can serve as a boundary maintaining mechanism (Bee, 1974, p. 98).

Within the Gypsy culture, boundary control takes the form of physical, psychological and cultural isolation.

The isolation may have begun even before the Gypsies left India. Through time several branches of the Gypsy nation developed; each branch known as a vitsa. When the vitsa grew too large it broke into smaller units called "kumpania". The smaller units made traveling easier. Since a smaller group would attract less attention it also helped them to survive with the meager resources available to them on the road. The vitsa is made up of extended families, with a common ancestor. The kumpania may be "a group of Rom traveling or living together in a territory, an economic and residential association" made up of several members of "extended cognatic family" units (Sutherland, 1975, p. 317) (See Figure 1). The vitsa represent the major social unit beyond the kumpania of the families. The kumpania are self-sufficient. They provide the Gypsies with social and cultural, as well as economic, security.

Vitsa members come together on a regular basis. This larger association serves to reestablish the lines of communication, enables the convening of the Kris (court), provides an opportunity for celebration, and maintains boundaries with the Gadjo. One of the more serious activities demanding attention during these gatherings is the arrangement of marriages. Parents can establish links with other members of the vitsa and negotiate possible marriages for their children with members of other kumpania. The system enables Gypsy intermarriage without inbreeding. This type of activity, regrouping into larger association, continues today but it is not as common as in the past, since the entire vitsa seldom comes together. It is less important today perhaps because of faster methods of communication and more frequent gatherings of smaller groups of vitsa members. In effect the Gypsies normally restrict these activities to other Gypsies.

In the past, because they traveled in small groups and generally stayed in one place only as long as it was lucrative to do so, they were less apt to be affected by alien cultures. The Rom usually established camps on the outskirts of villages

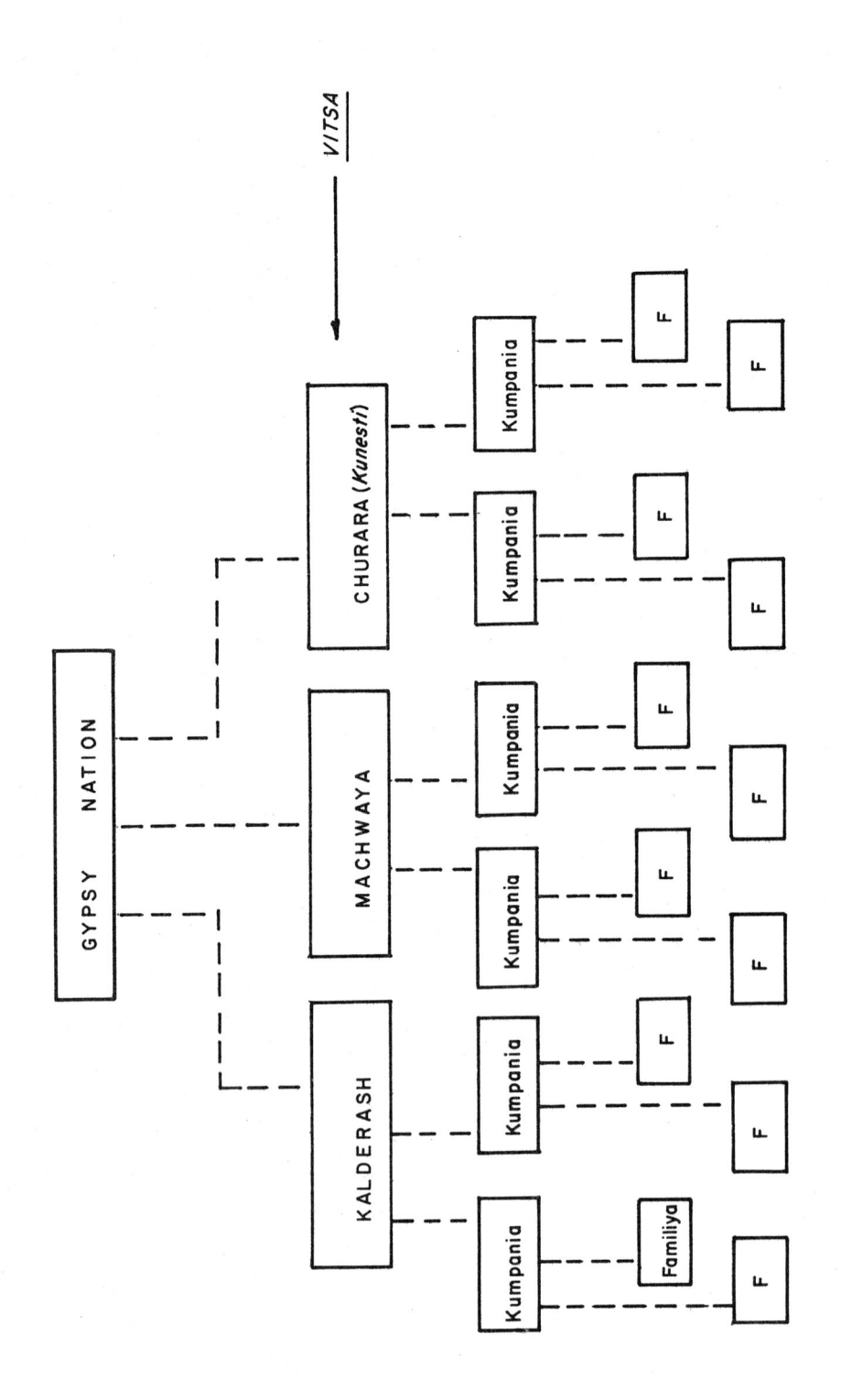

HIERARCHY OF GYPSY ASSOCIATION

Figure 1

and towns or in rural areas where there was grazing for their animals. The spatial separation coupled with the social distance produced an effective barrier to acculturation. (A discussion of distance between Gypsy groups is presented in Chapter IV under 'territoriality'.)

The socio-psychological isolation of the Gypsies stems from the mutual distrust between the Gypsies and the Gadjo. The Gypsies are aware of the prejudice against them, and the response is an equally vehement hostility toward the Gadjo. (It is impossible to tell whose prejudice came first.) This exclusionary practice fostered a resistance to anything which originates in the non-Gypsy culture. Alienation, and subsequently further resistance, is reinforced by incorporation of these prejudices into the Gypsy moral code.

The common accepted norms of behavior are different from those of the Gadjo. Moral taboos concerning many aspects of daily life, including washing, eating, dressing, sleeping, etc. strictly regulate Gypsy behavior. In the eyes of the Gypsy the Gadjo, who does not observe these rules of behavior, has made himself permanently unclean, and as such is excluded from participation with Gypsies in these activities. The boundary of physical separation is thus given a psychological justification.

The Gypsy regards eating as a semi-sacred activity, and believes that one should eat only with members of the same extended family and close friends. Meanwhile, a Gadjo will often sit at the same table with people he does not know. There are stories of Gypsies who would not allow Gadjo to touch or even wrap their food because the Gypsy thought the Gadjo to be a contaminating source. Today there is evidence of relaxation of these rules and the Gypsies are allowed to purchase and consume Gadjo convenience foods and supermarket goods (Cemeno, 1975). However, the concept of the unclean Gadjo persists strongly enough for most Gypsies to avoid any physical contact with non-Gypsies.

The established cultural norms in all cultures tend to produce barriers to personal interaction. Certain aspects of life, such as care of infants, personal hygiene or family interactions, are usually not directly experienced. Customs or characteristics may be preserved simply due to ignorance of an alternative. This is not to say that one culture is superior to another, but rather, differing values and prejudices reinforce the need to maintain rigid boundaries to prevent the corruption of that culture. This has led the Rom to deliberately maintain secrecy about themselves. In turn, the Gadjo reinforce this type of behavior by stereotyping the Gypsy as a mystic with supernatural powers. The Gypsy, in his role, becomes the manipulator and uses this as an opportunity to capitalize on the "stupid" Gadjo. Over the years the Gypsies have developed fortune-telling, card reading, spiritual advising and magic potions all designed to manipulate the Gadjo who would pay money for such "things". The Gypsies do not tell fortunes to other Gypsies. Yoors recounts a definition of fortune-telling given to him by a Gypsy woman, in which fortune-telling is seen as ". . . a vain and self-defeating search for expedient solutions to problems of moral integrity, and (is) caused by an unwillingness to face life as it (is)" (Yoors, 1967, p. 55).

Therefore, we have two cultural groups today, Gypsy and non-Gypsy, whose knowledge of one another is limited, or grossly distorted, and whose separation is maintained by boundaries produced by prejudice, negative reinforcement and deliberate physical and social isolation.

B. <u>Inflexible Internal Structure</u>

"Flexibility of internal structure refers to the culturally prescribed ranges of flexibility in such systematic aspects as status structure, the arrangement of groups vis-a-vis each other, or in the variability in the ways of acquiring political power" (Bee, 1967, p. 99). In other words, how closely are the institutions tied to one another; how rigid is the functioning of the system? It is generally held that autocratic systems under control of selected elites have a tendency to be very inflexible, allowing for little deviation from the traditionally established patterns of operation. In the Gypsy culture inflexibility in the internal structure is prevalent in both social and political institutions.

The rigid social rule, which discourages intermarriage, makes it extremely difficult for a non-Gypsy to be accepted into the group. The Gypsy who marries outside the "tribe" is usually expelled from the group. Intermarriage is one of the best indicators of acculturation. Kumpania are not usually located in close proximity, because an area will not support too large a Gypsy population due to their economic demands on an area. Since the process of arranged marriages is a practiced tradition among the Gypsies a father may travel considerable distances to acquire a spouse for his offspring. As a result there is a great deal of contact between vitsa members, in spite of the friction of distance, but not with the non-Gypsy population. Rigid social demands force the Rom to overcome external obstacles in order to satisfy his responsibilities in excluding outsiders.

The single most important element in Gypsy isolation is probably their language. Communication within the group is done through the medium of spoken Gypsy language. The use of Romanes efficiently separates the Gypsy culture and the Gadjo culture. The Gypsy knows just enough of the Gadjo language to operate on an economic level. On the other hand, the Gadjo does not know the Gypsy language. When no Gadjo are present only Romanes is spoken; Romanes is rarely spoken in the presence of a Gadjo. Consequently, not only is the language a medium for interpersonal communication for the Gypsy people, but it also has become a symbol of group solidarity and cultural identity.

A private communication device often used by the Gypsies is called the "Patrin". This is a sign language which can be compared to that used by other itinerant groups such as hobos or traveling salesmen. These signs are simply hieroglyphs which give directions or information to groups which may follow. A good example of the utility of this method of communication is given by Clébert:

> . . . a Gypsy woman will be the first to go into a farmhouse on the pretext of selling items of linen-drapery, or to tell fortunes. She operates so as to make the owner's wife talk, and she learns about important family matters--the number and ages of the children, recent illnesses and so forth. As she is going away, she will scratch on the wall or mark with chalk or charcoal signs which only her racial brothers will know how to make out. Some time later, when a

> second Gypsy woman shows up at the farm, she will have every opportunity to tell fortunes and reveal to the utterly amazed and therefore credulous farmer's wife details of their family life. (Clébert, 1970, p. 244)

The "Patrin" as a set of symbols is one example of the internalized self-sufficiency of the Gypsy culture. By establishment of various signs and symbols of communication the stability of the cultural system is reinforced (see Figure 2).

It is generally accepted by anthropologists that societies composed of closely-organized extended family units, as opposed to component biological families, are less apt to acculturate (Cotten, p. 276). The important element is the independence and self-sufficiency of the extended family.

> Each extended family is a miniature replica of the larger Gypsy society. The extended family is the nucleus of the band, just as the band is the nucleus of the tribe. Not only is it self-sufficient under ordinary circumstances but it can also be completely independent of the vitsa and of the other extended families. (Cotten, p. 276)

The power structure of the extended family is also replicated in the kumpania. The older dominant male makes the decisions for the family, often including either the other males in the family or the older dominant female. Age is highly respected by the Gypsies.

The leadership in the kumpania usually remains within one family. Any of the sons of a present leader may inherit the commanding role. However, he must have certain qualities. He must be mature and intelligent, thus commanding the respect and fear of the kumpania. Succession is of two types: the old leader dies in office, or is replaced by one of his sons while he is alive. Three conditions must be met for the leader to remain in

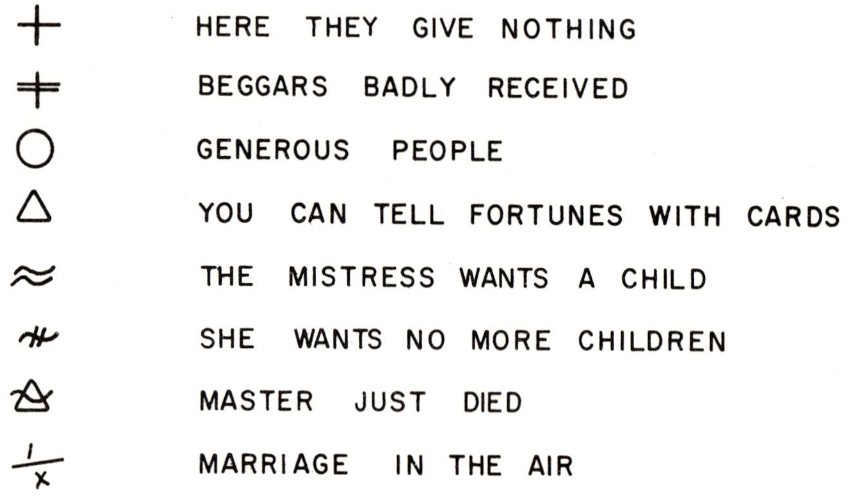

+	HERE THEY GIVE NOTHING
ⵜ	BEGGARS BADLY RECEIVED
○	GENEROUS PEOPLE
△	YOU CAN TELL FORTUNES WITH CARDS
≈	THE MISTRESS WANTS A CHILD
⚉	SHE WANTS NO MORE CHILDREN
◬	MASTER JUST DIED
1/x	MARRIAGE IN THE AIR

PATRIN

(EXAMPLES NOT ACCURATE - CLÉBERT, P. 244)

Figure 2

office. (1) He must not have broken any Gypsy rules. (2) He must not have gotten into trouble with the Gadjo. (3) He must continue to have full command of physical strength and mental powers. Removal is automatic if these conditions are not present.

The leader acts as judge in court trials, and is generally responsible for the behavior of the entire kumpania. Any infringements of political, economic, religious or social regulations are reported to his attention for correction or punishment.

Behavior of both males and females at all ages is maintained and regulated by traditional norms. The male is dominant in all levels of Gypsy society. Males are always served first at meals, the children second, and the women last. Material objects such as chairs or beds are occupied by men in order of their status within the family. The inflexible nature of relationships within Gypsy society, and the adherence to traditional behavior reduces the possibility of major changes within the Gypsy institutions.

C. <u>Self-correcting Mechanisms</u>

"Self-correcting mechanisms affect the ways in which the forces of conflict are balanced by forces of cohesion or togetherness" (Bee, p. 99). The success with which these two sets of forces are balanced within the system may determine whether or not the systems survive. Success of self-correcting systems may be indicated by such factors as the frequency of rule breaking by individuals of the system, by the frequency of unsettled disputes, or even the frequency of emigration from the system

(Bee, p. 100).

The fundamental agents which bind the extended families together into the vitsa, and serve to resolve conflicts, are the leaders and the council of elders. The leaders ". . . and the council serve to integrate the families in the matter of carrying out both the traditional rules and regulations and of adhering to any new ruling established by the council" (Cotten, p. 285). The political institutions, which handles the more complicated disputes of crimes, is the Gypsy court (Kris). The court is composed of a judge, the complainant, the defendant, the advocate and the jury. The court handles disputes which involve members of more than one extended family or kumpania. In the case of trials involving more than one vitsa, a leader from a third vitsa is selected as judge. The judge agrees to serve only after both parties swear to abide by his verdict.

The court is equipped to handle such crimes as murder, theft, mismanagement of funds, rape, divorce, and cases involving MaXrine (taboo or breaking of Gypsy law). Internal conflicts are handled almost exclusively within the Gypsy court system. Only as a last resort will Gadjo law or Gadjo courts replace the Gypsy courts. This is possible because of the nature of most disputes. Among the Gypsies the incidence of murder, theft and rape (i.e. serious crime) is very low. Most matters handled by the Gypsy courts are not generally regulated by Gadjo law. Getting into trouble with the Gadjo is obviously a different story. This requires banding together for the support of the accused against the Gadjo. The Kris is not only the mechanism for the resolution of conflict but it acts as a bonding agent for the group as a whole, while at the same time encouraging further separation from the Gadjo.

A personality trait which seems to have developed among Gypsies is the reduction of tension by the use of verbal argumentation. Much aggression is funneled into verbal confrontations which have become part of their lifestyle. When confronting Gadjo they are often arrogant, abusive and flagrantly emotional. At these times the behavior is both evasive for the Gypsy and frightening for the Gadjo. It serves to further increase the social distance while protecting the individuals from outsiders. It is an effective coercive device to use against a Gadjo, often permitting additional benefits for the Gypsy.

On the other hand, when Gypsies do not have the Gadjo with which to contend, this argumentative behavior becomes a form of verbal game, with little meaning in its content. In other words, statements which could completely destroy the self-esteem of a non-Gypsy, have little or no effect on the Gypsy. It would seem that this commonplace activity serves three functions as an individual's self-correcting mechanism. First, it acts as a pressure safety valve; all hostility and frustration can be released without harming oneself or other Gypsies. Secondly, it allows even the smallest Gypsy to assert dominance over others, building his own self-image and training him for future roles within Gypsy society. And thirdly, it teaches the Gypsy child a successful method of dealing with many Gadjo. What may seem to Gadjo as a manifestation of extreme conflict behavior is in actuality a mechanism for cohesion and identification for the Gypsy.

Immigration into the Gypsy society is almost impossible.

Emigration from the Gypsy society is equally rare, but not impossible. Once the Gypsy has left the tribe it is not likely that he will return, nor that he will be accepted should he wish to return. The practice of early arranged marriages and the especially strong motivation for children insure that most young people will continue the Gypsy way of life. One of the strongest cultural bonds among Gypsies is the desire to produce offspring and perpetuate the race. So strong is the pride of being Rom that most do not seriously consider emigrating from the community of Gypsies.

The persistence of a cultural system requires elements of identity characterized by maintenance of boundaries (real or imagined), rigid institutions and mechanisms for the resolution of conflicts. In examining these elements it can be seen that factors such as a language of private communication, standards of moral values, political organization to achieve group objectives and common norms of participation, all help to band the group together against attempts to incorporate them into the larger society.

II. Nature of the Contact Situation

The second major element in understanding Gypsy resistance to assimilation is the nature of the contact situation. The Gypsies have indeed been acculturated, but only to the degree necessary for survival and tolerated within their own cultural system. In the contact situation there is a set of potentially influential variables which could produce acculturation. The contact situation is where the transfer takes place; where the information about other systems is received. The events that occur during and after the contact will play an important role in rejection or acceptance of new ideas. The contact situation can be examined in numerous ways. Two useful methods view the nature of the contact situation in an ecological and a demographic context (Bee, p. 101).

The Gypsies are economically dependent on the non-Gypsy society. The one sphere in which Gypsy society is not self-sufficient is in providing self-generated income. This fact, more than any other, forces the Rom into a contact situation; they have no choice. The problem then becomes how to obtain money, goods and services with only minor loss of cultural identity.

The relationship between the Gypsy and his environment is quite superficial. He is interested only in obtaining what he needs or wants. There is no symbiotic relationship. Gypsies are not interested in Gadjo institutions or activities. The environment is to be used without regard to any repercussions within the Gadjo culture or systems. The Rom endeavor to utilize as many possible sources of income as possible. In this way, should a single source of income be lost, others will immediately fill the void. More importantly, the potentially overpowering influences of a single income source is substantially reduced, and likewise acculturation progresses only to a desired level. In other words, if a source becomes too dominating it can be discarded and another added in its place.

The very nature of the urban environment, with its anonymity and high densities, presents a broad economic base for the Rom. Size of the urban area and the complexity of its bureaucracy at times slow the processes within the system. As the Rom act upon elements in the urban system, the sheer size of that system is such that the eventual return of action on the Rom, through the same system, is delayed. By the time the system can react to the Rom there has been sufficient time for them to readjust or adapt to new influences. Thus, the larger the urban environment the more opportunity for the Rom to establish and reestablish income sources.

Two of the important demographic considerations in the contact situation are the relative size of the populations in contact, and the extent to which representation of the various demographic categories are involved in the contact. The primary contact with the Gadjo is made by the designated leader of the kumpania, whose power to manipulate the Gadjo institutions is his most important asset. He deals with the political structure and helps to establish new income sources, while protecting old sources. Because of the small size of the Gypsy population (in most areas it approximates one tenth of one percent), it is necessary for all age categories to interact in the contact situation. Everyone is expected to provide income for the family. The major contacts are made by mature Gypsy males. (Included in this group are "boys" between 15 and 20 years old. Because of earlier maturation and early marriages this age group must operate on a level similar to that of adults.) Other acculturation studies have shown that conflicts escalate when wives and children become involved in the contact situation. Gypsy women have very specialized and limited contact with Gadjo. Gypsy women are usually brought into contact with Gadjo through the welfare system. It is usually the women who provide information to the social worker in such a way as to insure continued support for the family. Gypsy women have become very skillful in their work. The other important source of contact for the women is in telling fortunes. This activity is usually done only in times of real necessity, and only by a few of the women today.

All other contacts, including those of the children, are on a very impersonal level and are quite superficial in nature. Children are taught very early in their lives how they are expected to handle the contact situation. As a result, the children often emulate the behaviors of their parents, often with rewarding success. A child's future is greatly enhanced if he or she exhibits "resourcefulness" at an early age.

The small size of the Gypsy population and their spatial dispersal throughout an urban area allows them to circulate freely in the urban environment, for the most part unnoticed by the Gadjo. It is the Gypsy who chooses the contact time and situation. This is a very important feature of the contact situation.

III. Conjunctive Relations

The contact situation is not actually contact between cultures but rather contact between individuals and small groups who establish communication links. "Intercultural roles" (SSRC Seminar, 1954, p. 980) are established between members of different cultures in a paired relationship. Reciprocity is implied by the linkage. The links established by Rom, with the exception of acquiring services such as medical aid, are almost solely economic. The three most important, in terms of useable income, are: "buyer-seller," "social worker-recipient," and "fortune teller-client". Each of these three inter-cultural roles requires some manipulative skill on the part of the Gypsy. Likewise, each of the reciprocal roles played by the Gadjo is very specialized and presents to the Gypsy a specific type of Gadjo. Neither the Gypsy nor the Gadjo will be completely representative of their respective cultures. However, these contacts do form the basis for the formulation of stereotypes for the entire alien culture.

The communication between the paired role players is both overt and at the same time very subtle. The more subtle transmission may often be the more important in the contact situation. The information transmitted by the Gypsy in all three of the above interactions is specific and restricted. A true picture of the whole cultural inventory is not presented through these paired relations. The exchanges are usually of brief duration and, more often than not, are not with the same Gadjo.

Ultimately, the Gypsy must accept some facet of the Gadjo culture as superior to his own before an acculturation could take place. This is rarely the case. In the economic sphere of the Gypsy's life, his methods work very well. The information transmitted from the Gadjo, whether he is a wholesale auto dealer, a female social worker, or a seeker of future events, will be reinterpreted by the recipient Gypsy. This filtering process is based on the prevailing Gypsy value system. The values expressed in the Gypsy value system are very different from those of the Gadjo, as was shown in discussing the persistence of the cultural system.

It is true that acceptance of Gadjo ideas and behaviors occurs quite often. However, it is usually the case that the acceptance is shallow and is used only in the contact situation rather than incorporated into the cultural system of the Rom.

IV. Cultural Processes Activated

Once an idea or trait has gained acceptance there are several alternative patterns of integration the element might assume.

A. Incorporation

". . . the donor's traits or ideas are integrated with the least possible disturbance to the recipient's preexisting system" (Bee, p. 105). The system itself remains virtually unchanged but the new traits are often modified to fit more easily into the system. Examples of incorporation among American Gypsies are the use of English and the imitation of selected Gadjo behaviors. Both of these adaptations are necessary in order to interact successfully with the Gadjo, but neither are necessarily used within the Gypsy social community. Another useful trait adopted by the Rom is the utilization of public assistance and other Gadjo institutions and organizations to supplement their income. In many cases it may be the only income for the family and is thus necessary for their survival. There is also more spatial integration with the Gadjo, although it is not clear if this is by choice as an adaptation, or simply the reaction to the housing market.

B. __Replacement__

". . . new elements are substituted for preexisting ones" (Bee, p. 105). In replacement the more affected items are those which make life easier and more simple for the Rom. Such things as keeping a fine automobile, wearing fashionable Gadjo clothing, utilizing consumer goods and supermarket foods, using Gadjo services (i.e. cleaners, drug stores, etc.), take out restaurants, and activities and items which can replace out of date items and give the Gypsy the appearance of wealth and prestige.

C. __Fusion__

". . . involves a combination or mixing of traits from two different cultural systems into a pattern which is different from either of them" (Bee, p. 106). The most obvious example of the fusion process is the change from nomadic lifestyle to the Gadjo settled lifestyle. The result has been a semi-settled population which has great intra-urban mobility with frequent inter-urban mobility. They are no longer nomadic, yet neither are they settled. An example of fusion in the Seattle area is the Gypsy Alternative School. Seattle is one of a handful of cities which have opened schools exclusively for Gypsies. The traditional American schoolroom situation is fused with the Gypsy culture to produce a classroom situation in which the Gypsy children who attend can progress at their own rate, surrounded by their own relatives and friends. They learn to read and write in English with a Gadjo teacher, but they are still unmistakably Gypsies.

D. __Isolation__

This is a pattern of non-integration in which traits are

held apart from the preexisting system and acceptance is in name only. This comprises much of the "acculturation" within the Gypsy society. The superficially incorporated traits and ideas are easily exchanged for new ones as necessity demands. It can be thought of as temporarily adapting to new environments. The pattern of non-integration of alien cultural traits corresponds to the impersonal nature of their contact situation.

V. Summary

It seems clear that the Rom have been able to resist assimilation into the larger Gadjo society because they have been able to adjust. They have adopted those elements into their culture which do not infringe upon their traditional beliefs. The Rom successfully use the surrounding urban Gadjo environment without sacrificing their cultural identity. This is accomplished by rigid external boundaries, institutions, and social structures. The opportunity of experiencing alternative patterns of behavior and beliefs is greatly reduced by limiting the types and degree of contact with the Gadjo. The self-sufficiency of the cultural system is the outstanding characteristic which largely accounts for non-assimilation.

CHAPTER 4
SOCIAL AND CULTURAL PROCESSES CREATING
SPATIAL PATTERNS AND BEHAVIORS

Today there is a Romani population whose social, economic, and cultural characteristics have been shaped through centuries of mobility, persecution, independence, and isolation from the host societies. Physical separation, wrought by political and physical barriers, enabled the Romani groups throughout the world to maintain the basic traditional behavioral norms and customs. The result has been a parallel development, or perhaps a parallel retention, of many of these basic patterns of behavior as a means to resist assimilation.

People are exposed to a variety of restrictions, either physical, cultural, social or psychological; restrictions which are either self-imposed or imposed from an external source. The type of restrictions and the methods used to deal with them may well determine how an individual grows and matures, and also how a particular culture evolves. Constraints upon one's life are very complex and interrelated. However, these constraints can be arranged into three general categories: environmental, temporal and spatial (see Figure 3).

Environmental constraints include the physical environment, as well as the psychological environments. They are defined by restrictions imposed by elements of culture, such as religion, economy and politics plus society itself. Temporal constraints

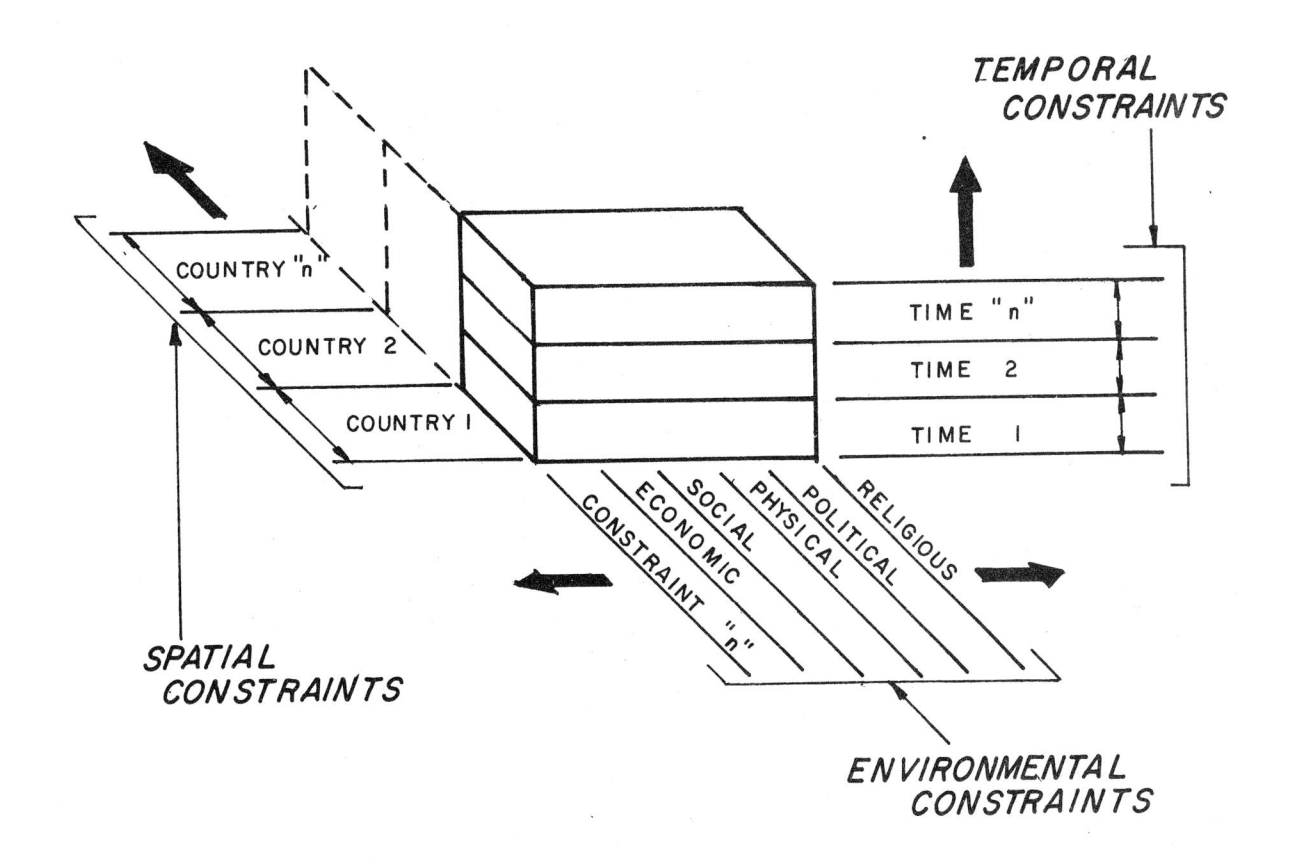

GENERALIZED DIAGRAM OF
CONSTRAINTS ON INDIVIDUAL FREEDOM

Figure 3

are reflected in changes through time. Restrictions will have differing degrees of impact according to the time at which they are imposed and their intensity and duration. The third kind of constraint is spatial. It refers to the constraints of location and arrangement in the space within which the group acts. The site of the environmental constraints affect a population at a particular time. Working simultaneously these three components constitute the frame of social interaction. Stability in the society is based on consistency of reactions to these constraints.

Gypsies must act as a group in a non-conforming manner in order to remain a distinct cultural entity or at least they must react differently than the host population. Some specific methods of interacting with Gadjo were discussed in the last chapter. It is possible to view these daily interactions on a more general level by examining the reaction of the Gypsies to the constraints they encounter.

The Romani culture as a system must effectively filter out the alien elements which could have detrimental effects. This is illustrated in Figure 4. An inner core, which represents basic traditions, beliefs, and behaviors of the culture is surrounded by an external sphere of insulation. The core experiences little acculturation but the zone of insulation is in constant motion making accommodative adjustments necessary for survival of the core in a hostile environment. By maintaining a defensive sociocultural buffer zone which separates all exclusive Gypsy functions from Gadjo functions, the rigid internal core can be preserved. External stress or excessive demands can be diverted or filtered before they reach the institutions they could harm.

ROMANI CULTURAL SYSTEM

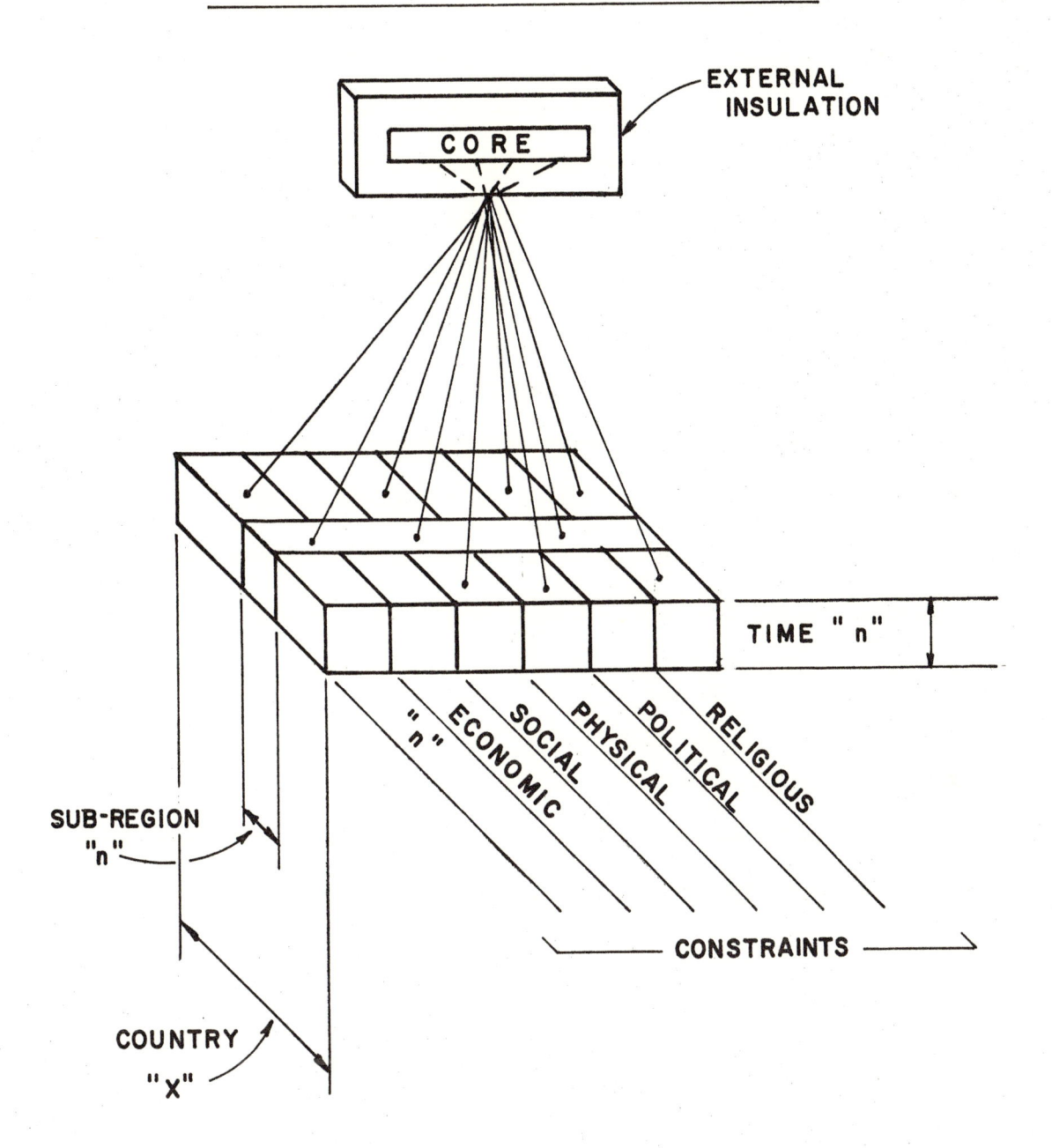

Figure 4

Likewise, by sustaining a rigid, inflexible core there is much greater flexibility in the insulation zone. Almost any type of adaptive change can be made without affecting the core as long as they remain separated. Thus, in essence, our discussion of the Romani culture should consider how the externalities are manipulated to allow the continuity of the internally desired functions.

The same social and cultural processes which stay in the way of the assimilation process and which handle the constraints imposed on the culture, also have spatial connotations. Many elements in the Romani culture can be analyzed within their spatial parameters. In fact, the Romani culture, by virtue of its separation from the Gadjo, allows us to observe more easily the spatial consequences of social behavior. Explaining the uniqueness of the Gypsy lifestyle is therefore not the only goal of the research. In addition, we can gain insight from the realization that the behaviors of the Rom, as well as ourselves, do indeed produce patterns in space.

Four elements which appear to be very important in the Romani lifestyle will serve to illustrate how spatial patterns are expressed dynamically in the Romani culture. Even though related as components of a complex whole, each of the four (territoriality, communication, mobility, and consumership) will be analyzed and illustrated independently.

A. Territoriality

The concept of territoriality may at first seem to be incongruous when discussing the Gypsies. Are they not the people who have no territory of their own; no homeland; no Zion? It is of course true that the Gypsies have no physical territory which belongs exclusively to the Romani nation, and thus no symbolic attachment to a particular place. Yet the Gypsies, with their own identity, can and are attached or associated with "anyplace" they happen to be at a particular time (Sopher, p. 108). The Gypsies as a group have very special economic demands because of the occupations they have chosen. These include such income sources as automobile dealing, fortune-telling, gambling, welfare, and other government subsidies, plus various and assorted self-employed undertakings. With little imagination one can see that these specialized income sources impose rigid locational constraints in order to be used continuously by a large population. Great care must be taken not to exceed the economic carrying capacity of an area so that the sources of income will not be prematurely exhausted. The territorial behavior of the Rom is directly related to their economic survival.

The cultural core demand for defined territory is the perpetuation of the vitsa. All Gypsies realize the precariousness of their type of economic situation. It is of the utmost importance for this freely mobile population to be in relatively constant communication especially in regard to spatial arrangements. Workable methods for attributing space to members of the groups must be maintained (Eisenberg, p. 223). This is done mainly through the adherence to a home range coupled with mutual avoidance behavior between Gypsy groups (Eisenberg, p. 223). The establishment of territory thus becomes a social function. The association and identification of a kumpania with a specific area is socially rather than locationally determined. A kumpania can operate in almost any territory as long as that territory is not already occupied by another kumpania. The important consideration is not the site location but rather the location relative to other groups.

Informal establishment of a territory seems to be on a first come first serve basis. Many of the Gypsies in the Seattle-Tacoma area have been in the Northwest twenty to thirty years. This in no way implies that they have remained in the same locations for this length of time. There is a great deal of change in the composition of the Gypsy population, as we shall see later.

Settling of a kumpania in a particular area implies that the group members have control of the local income sources. The leader or spokesman of the kumpania may in many cases have created some of the resources available to the group. This in turn raises his position within the group, and often allows him to collect additional income for himself by charging a commission to members for sharing the source he has created. The leader, for his part, may also provide some measure of protection to members against newcomers or other incursions on the source (Hinde, p. 393). Local police can also be used for protection of a vitsa by allowing only a small number of business licenses or enforcing regulations only on newcomers. Should a leader lose or misappropriate a major source of income he may find himself in trouble within his kumpania or his vitsa. He may even be replaced by another, who is in better standing with the local Gadjo. The importance of the leader as the symbol of the core makes it imperative for him not to break any Gypsy laws or get into trouble with the Gadjo if he wishes to remain in a power situation within his kumpania.

Washington State has at least four large kumpania, occupying four areas: Seattle, Tacoma, Everett, and Spokane. All of these groups are well established and semi-permanent, with kinship ties between them. Each has its own way of dealing with the Gadjo, and each group has used similar methods from time to time. One example which illustrates this point is the use of academicians and education. The leaders in Spokane, Seattle, and Tacoma have all sought and received either state or federal funding for schooling their children (*Seattle Times*, April 18, 1968). The only segregated school for Gypsies still in operation today is in Seattle. The other two have been closed because of mismanagement of funds, poor attendance or through difficulties with the Gadjo political bureaucracy. The Spokane group now has an anthropologist working on their behalf, and the Tacoma group has a linguist attempting to obtain funds for continued research on the Gypsy language.

The significance here is that leaders often emulate the success of other groups, and at present are using the academic community in order to supplement kumpania incomes through various funding programs. The groups are not only using the same sources of income in their respective territories, but also in some cases, inadvertently perhaps, competing for the same funds. There is also competition with other minority groups as well.

The concept of territory for the Gypsies refers to a functional area of their activities. The territory is neither exclusive nor clearly demarcated. The group which resides in the particular area at a particular time uses the territory to derive its livelihood and economic support. Functional distance within the group and within its territory is maintained by the leadership, by family ties, and by cooperative linkages between group members. The territorial domain of one Gypsy group excludes other Gypsies from this territory at any given time though it does not preclude the use of the same territory by subsequent users.

B. Communication

The preservation of Romanes discussed earlier is significant also for the assessment of the communication system. A language is retained only if it is used and considered important by the group. The Gypsies exclude all Gadjo from their communication system simply by speaking Romanes. This exclusivity is achieved with Gypsies conversing on the street corner or talking over long distance on the telephone. The language also allows an extra degree of freedom of movement between Gypsy groups. All Rom, regardless of their location, speak Romanes and a stranger's status is immediately established when he speaks.

We have seen the importance of communication for the maintenance of spatial boundaries; but the communication system plays other important parts in the lifestyle of the Gypsies. Three important core demands are manifested in the communication system: The preservation of Romanes as a separate language for elementary social communication between Gypsies; the maintenance of contacts for future marriage contracts; and a reliable network for the diffusion of information regarding births, deaths, festivals or other significant events which may require traveling to another location. The information system must be able to function in times of stress as well as times of leisure. Romanes as the language of the Gypsies has become the communication medium for both basic needs (i.e. the daily interactions between Gypsies) and the exceptional needs (i.e. unusual or irregular events).

All significant communication among the Rom is oral. The information system has special mechanisms which enable the Gypsies to maintain the maximum in verbal communication. In a country the size of the United States it would have been impossible, given the dispersal of the Romani groups, to have accomplished the three core demands by face to face contact were it not for two technical devices which extend the reach of direct communication: the automobile and the telephone. Both of these devices are necessary means for the operation of the verbal communication network of the highly mobile Rom.

Yoors describes incidents in which Gypsies used the telephone to relay messages before World War I in Europe as well as in the United States (Yoors, p. 87). Today the telephone constitutes the most important means to maintain contact between individuals and groups. It is not unusual for a Gypsy family to have telephone bills which range as high as $700 to $1000 in one month. Telephones are easy to obtain and easy to leave behind. As the telephone has become more sophisticated, its use has been simplified. Dial a number and the world can be opened in a few brief moments. The telephone conveniently meets the communication needs of the Rom.

The automobile is only slightly less important, although in many cases it would be difficult to rank the order of importance. Mobility is an essential aspect of a Rom's lifestyle. Fast luxurious cars make travelling very appealing to the Rom. Visitors are welcomed in the Gypsy household not only because they have been away for a time, or they live in another area, but also since they bring news and valuable information from other parts of the Country. Trips to visit relatives, attend funerals or weddings, to celebrate slava or pomani[1] all become opportunities to renew social connections and disseminate information. Not only is the automobile a useful instrument for communication, but it is also a financial asset which can be carried along on the moves. The car is an efficient investment which is easily retrieved, usually with a profit.

An illustration of how these two devices, the telephone and the automobile, help the Rom fulfill their cultural responsibilities is the hospitalization of a Rom. This phenomenon has been observed by many Gadjo but probably understood by few. Roles and behavioral norms are well established among the Rom. Serious illness or an operation is considered an appropriate cause for a gathering of the clan. Friends and relatives are notified by telephone; at this point the socialization process begins. As many friends and relatives of the patient, who are able to gather, do so. Within a day or two, Gypsies arrive at the hospital from all over the country. Some may use an airline but most will arrive by car. The Gypsies crowd into the hospital, take over the lobby, hallways, lawns or whatever, and they stay until the Romani patient is released from the hospital or dies. The mass communication of the event has produced a significant spatial response.

The same event can also illustrate the importance of communication between Gypsy and Gadjo. As might be expected the hospital personnel have their hands full. Not only must the staff deal with an invasion of Gypsies, but also go about their own duties while securing hospital property and calming the Gadjo patients who have become fearful of their live and possessions. (These fears are generally unfounded but are nevertheless real.) The Gypsies would prefer to stay in the patient's room, but this is not possible. Instead arrangements are usually made between the director of the hospital and the Gypsy leaders to restrict the gathering to the lobby or other location, while allowing two or three visitors with the patient.

Since the Gadjo does not understand why all the Gypsies are camping at the hospital, he is easily conned into believing that the patient is a Gypsy king, queen, prince or princess. This is a common story used by Gypsies and it generally works, even the newspapers add their credence to the story. The royal personage is of course the object of homage for the attending Gypsies. With royalty at their humble hospital how could they possibly evict the reverent pilgrims? (Salloway, p. 120). The way the Gypsy communicates to the Gadjo, and the response received, often reinforces the stereotypic images of both parties.

The importance of the communication network in cultural processes is also found in the arrangement of marriages. Marriage contracts for children are arranged by their fathers.

Negotiations extend for as long as two, three, or more years. The procedure is a rather formalized and traditional affair which can occupy much time and energy.

Successful marriage arrangements must secure not only the happiness of marriage for their children, but also secure the economic and political future of the fathers, which may be greatly affected by their choice of marriage partners. Marriages usually occur between members of different kumpania at separate locations and at substantial distances. A great deal of information is needed about the young people before the final agreement can be reached. For this information all sources are utilized: friends, relatives and often rumors and gossip all pass valued information to the negotiators.

The groom's father offers a price he feels the bride is worth, depending on her virginity and her future potential. If she appears to be an asset to her husband and seems able to support her future family she will bring a higher price. The bride's father may turn down the offer if he feels the girl is worth more, or if the future family is not acceptable to him. This mediation is done in face to face negotiation and may require the groom's father to make several trips to the location of the bride.[2]

A number of issues are at stake here. Marriages affect relationships between the kumpania. Future communication and interaction depend on good marriages and new large families. Communication linkages established between fathers become the starting point for the other social, cultural, and economic exchanges among Gypsy groups.

C. Mobility

Spatial mobility among Gypsies is considerably different than among non-Gypsies. Movement is a part of their culture. It serves many purposes. Gypsies respond to stress or financial difficulty in an area with relocation. Mobility has been a part of the Gypsy lifestyle throughout the ages. Today it is much more likely that the Rom will live in one place more or less permanently. However, the establishment of a home base does not commit him to stay there; indeed, what may seem to the Gypsy as permanent may be perceived by the Gadjo as nomadic.

Spatial mobility in Romani groups can be categorized into three major types: I. inter-city migration; II. intra-city change in residence; and III. inter-regional circulation.

I. Inter-city Migration

Residential movement between urban centers is a frequent occurrence among the Rom. It usually takes the form of a chain migration in which families join an existing vitsa in a different location. They in turn send information back to the origin, often creating additional migration to the new kumpania. One important cause of migration and the consequent redistribution of the Gypsy population is marriage.

The new bride joins her husband's family; in most cases this means changing kumpania and site location. In time, the new husband and wife are able to support themselves and no longer need rely on the husband's family for financial support. This occurs most often after the first child is born to the couple. At this time the new family may stay with the husband's family, move to another location within the same area, or perhaps relocate in another city in a kumpania where they have relatives. The constant rearrangement of the Gypsy population through marriage and breaking off of the smaller biological family complicates the controlling of a particular territory while it increases the need for social communication between the Gypsy groups.

Marriage, financial problems, legal entanglements with the Gadjo, establishment of new territory and stress within the Gypsy community are the most common reasons for inter-city migration. As the Gypsy community becomes more stable (i.e. sets up income sources and establishes relations with Gadjo in the area) there seems to be a trend toward less migration between cities and more relocation within a particular urban area.

II. Intra-city Change in Residence

The choice of a family's residence is influenced by internal as well as external forces. Internal forces are the needs and expectations of the household: size of family, location relative to other Gypsies, and location relative to income sources. External forces are environmental: neighborhood, dwelling type, market, relative location in the urban space. The major demand is separation from the Gadjo population. By locating in the proximity of other Gypsies, socialization may occur easily. Segregated neighborhoods or ethnic enclaves are not generally established; residential integration within the Gadjo neighborhoods helps to conceal the Gypsies as a separate subgroup of the population.

The attraction of specific areas of the city change over time. The powerful elements for drawing families to an area are first, the availability of economic resources and second, proximity to other Gypsies for social interaction. Changes in these two components coupled with stressful encounters with Gadjo account for most of the intra-urban relocation. The relative ease with which the Rom become mobile makes it difficult for the Gadjo system to operate efficiently when it deals with the Gypsies.

The Rom may change residence once or twice a year, or they may stay in the same location for longer periods if they do not experience hardships. Gypsies prefer to live in houses which have been previously occupied by Gypsies. The Rom who own homes invariably rent to other Gypsies. Thus, the location of houses used by Gypsies do not change often even though these houses experience frequent changes of occupants.

III. <u>Inter-regional Circulation</u>

The most common type of mobility employed by the Rom is inter-regional. Generally, the home base is established in a favored area. Family groups may be traveling as much as sixty percent of the time (Sutherland, p. 47). Many travel for economic reasons such as purchasing or selling cars or other goods. Traveling is also a "social imperative and is incorporated into the whole structure of law, social control, morality and religious beliefs" (Sutherland, p. 49). It has symbolic meaning as well. Gypsies believe that travel is necessary for health and good luck, while staying in one place promotes sickness and bad luck (Sutherland, p. 51).

Traveling is used as an effective method for solving disagreements between families. The families simply leave their home area until such time as they can return in peace. Thus pressures from the Gypsy community as well as from the Gadjo community can be relieved easily. Demands from the police department, governmental authorities, schools, neighbors or landlords can be met by an exodus of the family (Sutherland, p. 50).

For the most part travel today is for economic or social purposes. Less frequently, but still of great importance, travel is used as a political or problem solving device. Most of the travel is between states or between regional areas, and may span a few days to several weeks depending on the purpose. With few exceptions this inter-regional traveling is done by automobile.

D. Consumership

Gypsy consumer methods are different than those of other minority groups. The key aspect of Gypsy consumership patterns is immediacy. When faced with rejection, long waiting periods, disparaging remarks, or second rate treatment while shopping, the Gypsy responds by going elsewhere to get what he wants. The response of other "disadvantaged groups" in this society are less flexible than that of the Gypsy (Salloway, p. 113). When faced with these problems their response may be retreat which results in alienation and rejection of the system. They may be less inclined to penetrate the system again (Salloway, p. 125). This was found to be especially true in medical care utilization (Salloway, p. 113). The Gypsy lives in a world of hostility toward Gadjo and accepts discrimination as "normal"; he does not like it, but he can deal with it effectively.

Culture provides an explanation of Gypsy consumer behavior. Their spatially irrational consumer patterns can be interpreted by investigating underlying causes. The core goal of the Gypsy behavior is to perpetuate the Gypsy race and lifestyle.

The Gypsy must operate in the Gadjo world to satisfy his needs. This Gadjo system is based on the assumption that all consumers are literate. The consumer reads labels, advertising and instructions. This would seem to make the illiterate Gypsy disadvantaged, but it is not generally the case. The success of the Rom in obtaining desired services testifies to the usefulness of their social system. The compensating factor in consumership is the communication network of the Rom.

In their search for alternatives, Gypsies often find the location of the best goods or services for the least price through trial and error. They also find the places where Gypsies are welcomed or treated well. The information is gathered, stored and then recycled through the communication network. Businesses, hospitals and other suppliers often find themselves serving more and more Gypsies as the information spreads through the network.

Gypsies often travel great distances for a service which they feel is not available nearby. Where a Gadjo would be willing to pay a higher price or have lesser quality rather than travel afield, a Gypsy is not so willing. This implies that he is actually aware of a better alternative elsewhere or simply that he is so dependent on his social system that he is unaware of an equal opportunity closer to home.

Gypsies seek and often demand high quality goods and services and are quite willing to shop around until they have found what they expect.

E. Summary

The objective of this chapter was to analyze the response to constraints on the American Gypsy population by examining behavioral elements which have spatial connotations. Territoriality, communication, mobility, and consumership all have spatial dimensions which characterize the Gypsy lifestyle.

Romani culture consists of two parts, an inflexible aspatial core, and a highly flexible external periphery. The core remains stable and relatively unaffected while the external periphery changes rapidly. The maintenance of two separate parts allows continuity and the development of a cohesive complex which is generally impervious to external encroachments by the host society. Each of the four behavioral elements is viewed as having demands in the core region to maintain cultural norms, and in the periphery or buffer zone to adapt to environmental stimuli. The Gypsies as a group have been successful at balancing these sometimes conflicting demands.

Utilization of space is based on the social and cultural values and needs of a population. It is clear that Gypsies have different attitudes and perform different activities than do Gadjo in the same urban space. Analyzing the use of space aids in discovering the underlying social and cultural processes which operate in the Gypsy culture.

FOOTNOTES--CHAPTER IV

[1] *Slava* are feasts which celebrate family saints' day and *pomani* is the yearly feast for the dead (Sutherland, 1975, p. 318-319).

[2] Marriage arrangements are discussed in several publications. See Gropper (p. 123), Yoors (p. 182), Clébert (p. 211), and Cohn (p. 49).

CHAPTER 5

SEATTLE ROM

In the Seattle SMSA there are approximately 150 to 200 Gypsies. Throughout the year the number fluctuates by 20 to 50 persons as Rom travel in and out of the area. The Seattle Rom conform rather closely to the characteristics and attitudes of the Gypsy population in the United States presented in earlier chapters. There are, however, several significant differences which, in the long run, could have profound impacts on the Seattle Rom and thus produce repercussions on other Gypsy groups in the United States.

I. History

The Seattle Rom share their history with other Gypsy groups in America. Physiological or linguistic studies of Seattle Rom do not substantiate beyond doubt the origins of the group; yet physical characteristics and mother tongue do differentiate the Seattle Rom from the Gadjo. Seattle Rom believe that they originate from Romania, but they have little knowledge of the relative location of Romania or India (Cemeno, 1976). Their limited acquaintance with both geography and time sequence make direct questioning about origin a fruitless pursuit. Suffice it to say, they identify themselves as Gypsy and are believed to have the same historical lineage as other Rom in the United States.

A significant number of Gypsies have been living in Seattle since the early 1950's (*Seattle Times*, May 2, 1962). There has been a more or less constant turnover in population. More recently, perhaps the last five years, the Romani community has stabilized. Many have, for the present, settled semi-permanently in Seattle. Most of the Rom still travel frequently, using Seattle as a home base. During the past year the travel pattern seems to closely approximate that quoted by Sutherland for a group of Rom in Barvale, California. Households with an elderly person or couple at the head, studied over a nine-month period, indicated that 26% of their time was spent in travel. On the other hand, households with a young couple at the head traveled 56% of the time (Sutherland, p. 5).

At least ten families (fifty-one individuals) have been Seattle residents for the last four years, and half of these families own their own homes.

II. Resistance to Assimilation

A. Cultural System

The Seattle Rom like other Rom in America hold strongly the desire to perpetuate their race and social isolation. The same boundary maintaining mechanisms discussed in Chapter III prevail in Seattle today. Social activities are restricted to the Rom in-group. The concept of the extended family as the important social unit seems widely held by the Seattle Rom. There is almost no interaction between Gypsy and Gadjo at the personal level. (One notable exception is a recent marriage of a Gypsy boy and a Gadji. She has been accepted by the Gypsies because she will hopefully produce Gypsy children. The degree of real social acceptance is still unknown.)

Norms of behavior, such as aggressiveness and coercion, which promote the maintenance of boundaries are easily recognized in Seattle Gypsy encounters with Gadjo. Interaction with Gadjo is limited to economic situations including both interaction to supply income and interaction to purchase and/or supply goods and services. Most boundary maintenance mechanisms continue throughout the life stages.

The Seattle Romani population adhere to the inflexible internal structure evidenced in other Romani groups (Yoors, p. 172). Marriages are arranged for children at an early age, usually by the time they are 15. In the past year (June 16, 1975 to June 16, 1976) there were four marriages in Seattle and environs. With the exception of one Gadji marriage, all of the marriage partners were Gypsy. It is not uncommon for Gypsy men in Seattle to have close physical relationships with Gadjo women, but it is rare for the Gypsy to marry the Gadji.

In the home only Romani is spoken if a Gadjo is not present. English is the second language, and most of the Rom have only a minimum of understanding above the "street" level.

Informal leadership among Seattle Rom has been rigid until recently. Within the last year the local leader proved to be less than desirable when funds directed for the entire Gypsy community were pocketed. Dissonance grew and eventually the internal organization, of which the outsiders in Seattle know very little, except that it does exist, forced the leader to relinquish his power to another Gypsy. The new leader has stabilized relations within the community and effectively reestablished creditability with the Gadjo institutions. The replacement of a recognized leader was carried out within the political system of the Rom. Even though the change was external to the Gadjo political system, the decision was a foregone conclusion since the new leader is the only person with a previously established working relationship with the Seattle welfare office. The choice is consistent with evidence referred to in the literature; the person with the most power and influence within Gadjo society ideally makes the best leader for the Gypsy community because of the Gypsy dependence on the Gadjo economic system.

In Seattle there are elements of three known vitsa: the Kalderash, the Machways, and the Kuneshti (part of the Churara vitsa). The extent of their political organization has not been verified through this research. There is some friction between the groups, but there would seem to be no significant hostility or competition in the Seattle area. Reportedly (*Seattle Post Intelligencer*, February 4, 1973), the Kalderash were the majority in Seattle during the 1950's but more recently there are either fewer Kalderash in the area, or the Rom are beginning to make less distinction between the vitsa.

The self-correcting mechanisms also exist in Seattle. However, they are not easily witnessed by Gadjo since they are internal to the Gypsy community. The existence of the different vitsa and the limiting of ingress and egress strongly suggest internal mechanisms which help to stabilize the Romani community while maintaining separation from Seattle Gadjo.

Most of the mechanisms which hinder the process of assimilation are in evidence in the Seattle area. Social separation of the Gypsies is complete while the outward appearance of physical integration is maintained. This fact, of course, helps the Rom to preserve some anonymity among Gadjo. By remaining aloof from Gadjo interactions, the Seattle Rom can carry on their special types of self-employment with little interference from the outside. As long as the Rom can continue to perpetuate the more traditional occupations of the Rom, so too they can continue to identify with their own cultural heritage.

B. <u>Contact Situation and Conjunctive Relations</u>

The Seattle Rom seem to have virtually the same contact situation as the Rom in other parts of the country. There is superficial contact at all age levels (Sutherland, p. 67; Gropper, p. 32). The urban environment, the small size of the Gypsy social community and the economic dependence of the Rom on the Gadjo system, forces most Rom to interact daily with Gadjo. Often these encounters simply reinforce the desirability of remaining Gypsy. Rom consistently meet prejudice, distrust and avoidance.

Once a month on average, many Gypsies visit the Seattle Auto Auction. Here they purchase and sell late model automobiles. They have a strong preference for large, expensive cars which can bring large gains at sale. The contact with Gadjo at the auction is both cordial and at the same time patronizing. The Gypsies are in business to make the best possible deal, and to this end they have become skillful buyers and suppliers of automobiles.

Many of the Gypsy men and boys spend a great deal of time soliciting auto dealerships for unwanted cars. It is often possible to buy a car wholesale from a dealer and resell through newspaper advertisements or on the street--often with a considerable profit. In short, the major contact situation which involves the men in Seattle is through the transfer of automobiles. This activity is self-employing and since the Gypsy is in control of the confrontation, poses little threat to cultural assimilation.

The Gypsy women in Seattle are in charge of the family. They are expected (from an early age) to have many children and to help in the support of the family. They do not appear to contribute greatly to the family income. This is contrary to the role played by women cited by both Sutherland and Gropper. In both of these studies the women are the major breadwinners; bringing in money for the routine daily expenditures. One of their major roles is to handle the social worker from the welfare office. In Seattle more often it is the men who maintain contact with the Gadjo. The role of women in economic relations is rather limited. The reason is yet to be discovered, but I speculate that life and the search for economic gain is less demanding in Seattle than elsewhere, thus giving the men more free time and removing the necessity for women to manipulate the welfare people. This limited involvement of the women in economic activities provides them with excess idle time.

Seattle Gypsy women, of course, have some contact with Gadjo, usually women, through "spiritual advising". At least four Gypsy women in Seattle provide their services to the public in the form of card reading, palmistry or other methods of "fortune telling". The act of telling or purchasing a fortune is a misdemeanor in Seattle (Seattle City Ordinance No. 12.11.240). To avoid conflict with the law Gypsies have simply labeled what they do as "spiritual advising". One woman has even obtained a Seattle city license using it as an advertising gimmick. However, it has little relevancy to the profession since for a fee a license can be obtained for just about anything. In other words there is no definition for spiritual advising at the licensing bureau and thus no specified duties or activities which are regulated by the license. The same woman has also opened a second "office" in Bellevue, a Seattle suburb. All of these women work out of their homes. Store fronts are no longer used in Seattle and the charge is normally ten to fifteen dollars for a ten minute reading. (They will take less if necessary and more if possible.) As in other areas, the art of fortune-telling in Seattle is usually practiced in times of stress or when there is a need for additional income. Advertisements are placed in daily newspapers, on handbills, in local community newspapers and even in the University newspaper (see Figure 5). One woman who lives outside the city limits has a large billboard in the front yard of her home.

The methods used by Seattle fortune tellers are similar to those used elsewhere by other Gypsies (Gropper, p. 41; Maas, p. 80). Business generally seems good in Seattle and more of the women, who have little to do during the day, are entering the market when an opportunity arises. Gypsy women who tell fortunes contribute to the family income. The activity allows the

MRS. ANITA
Spiritual and psychic tarot card reader, adviser on all problems regarding business, love, marriage, and family problems. 784-1781
(400-A-53)

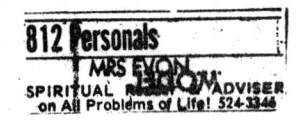

812 Personals
MRS EVON
SPIRITUAL READER ADVISER
on All Problems of Life! 524-3346

SPIRITUAL READER & ADVISOR
There is no problem so great that she can't solve. Tell you how to hold your job when you have failed and how to succeed. Will listen to your troubles and tell you what to do about them. Re-unites the separated. One visit will convince you she has power. Phone 525-1770.

LITTLE NICKEL

GREENWOOD ADDITION

Miss Evon E.S.P.
Reader and Advisor
Advice given on all walks
Of Life: Love, Marriage,
Business, etc.
Also, card reading.
Open daily 9AM–8PM.
For appt. call:
524-3346
All readings private
And confidential.

812 Personals
MRS EVON...
BACK FROM VACATION
Spiritual Reader
ADVICE given on all problems of life. She asks no questions, but qualified to answer any of yours. All readings private & confidential. Licensed Reader. For Appt. Call 524-3346   Hrs. 9am-8pm

HAVE YOU HAD your cards read lately? Experienced, accurate, on bus line. Please call 783-4989.

UNIVERSITY OF WASHINGTON
DAILY

812 Personals
—Mrs. Evon—
Spiritual Reader
and Advisor
Advice given on all problems of life — such as love, marriage, business, etc. There is no problem so great that she cannot solve it. She asks no questions, but is able to answer any of yours. One visit will convince you! All readings private & confidential. Private consultations— also group readings & parties. For an appointment call: in Bellevue area, 454-7091; in Seattle area, 524-3346. Hours 9 am to 9 pm.

SEATTLE TIMES

SEATTLE GYPSY FORTURE TELLING ADVERTISEMENTS

Figure 5

women to liberate themselves from their male dominated society through relationships with Gadjo in which they can assert themselves by controlling the contact situation and in turn reinforce their superiority over the Gadjo (Okley, p. 20).

In the contact situations between Gadjo and Gypsy in Seattle specific roles are adopted by the Gypsy. Interaction is normally initiated by the Gypsy. Communication between these Gypsies and Gadjo is more often superficial and manipulative on the part of the Gypsy. The impersonal nature of the contact has led to further cultural and social isolation of the two groups in Seattle.

C. Assimilation Processes Activated

The integration of alien traits among Seattle Gypsies generally takes the forms already discussed; namely, (a) incorporation, (b) replacement, (c) fusion, and (d) isolation. The degree to which these forms of integration traits are expressed in the Seattle population is impossible to determine without extensive longitudinal study. Each of the types is outwardly visible in the general behavior patterns which can be observed.

a) Incorporation: Seattle Gypsies use English as a second language in all contacts with Gadjo. A second incorporation is the use of welfare institutions to supplement family income.

b) Replacement: The most obvious replacement of preexisting traits with new ones is the use of the automobile and the reliance on consumer goods.

c) Fusion: The two cultural systems have been fused into new patterns of semipermanent residence in Seattle. This has been accompanied by a high rate of intra-urban migration.

d) Isolation: The most prevalent form of isolation is the continual rejection of Gadjo social relationships by Seattle Gypsies.

The integration of traits progresses at a slow rate in most cultures. There is a great deal yet to be learned about measuring the rate, degree, and permanence of adopted alien traits among Gypsies.

III. Social and Cultural Processes Which Create Spatial Patterns and Behaviors

The Seattle Romani population operates as a distince subset within the larger Seattle population. It will be helpful to examine some of the basic socioeconomic characteristics of our Gypsy population to better understand the social and cultural influences which function in this separate community.

Table 5 was compiled using personal interviews and 1970 census data. Thirty-two Gypsy families (147 individuals) were used in the sample. This table compares the absolute number in each population by age cohort and gives the percentage in each cohort within the total population. The same information, converted to percentages, was then used to construct the two population pyramids in Figure 6.

Comparison of the two pyramids show some dramatic differences between the two populations. The pyramid for Seattle is

TABLE 5

AGE COHORT DISTRIBUTIONS FOR SEATTLE GYPSIES AND SEATTLE GADJO

Cohort	Male Gypsy	Male Seattle	Female Gypsy	Female Seattle	Total Male-Female Gypsy	Total Male-Female Seattle	% of Total Pop. Gypsy	% of Total Pop. Seattle
0-4	8	17,949	9	17,045	17	34,994	11.6	6.6
5-9	10	18,537	16	17,862	26	36,399	17.7	6.9
10-14	11	20,056	18	19,404	29	39,460	19.7	7.4
15-19	7	21,904	11	23,426	18	45,330	12.2	8.5
20-24	4	26,896	6	31,631	10	58,527	6.8	11.0
25-29	2	17,757	4	15,900	6	33,657	4.1	6.3
30-34	5	17,757	9	15,900	14	33,657	9.5	6.3
35-39	7	12,548	4	12,779	11	25,327	7.5	4.8
40-44	2	12,548	5	12,779	7	25,327	4.8	4.8
45-49	2	15,985	1	17,711	3	33,696	2.0	6.4
50-54	2	15,985	3	17,711	5	33,696	3.4	6.4
55-59	0	15,531	0	17,091	0	32,622	0	6.1
60-64	1	13,388	0	15,097	1	28,485	0.7	5.4
65-69	0	8,475	0	11,813	0	20,288	0	3.8
70-74	0	8,475	0	11,813	0	20,288	0	3.8
75+	0	10,602	0	18,475	0	29,077	0	5.5
Totals	61	254,393	86	276,437	147	530,830	100.0	100.0

SOURCE: Sample taken from Seattle Gypsy population, 1976; data for Seattle population from U. S. Census, 1970.

Figure 6

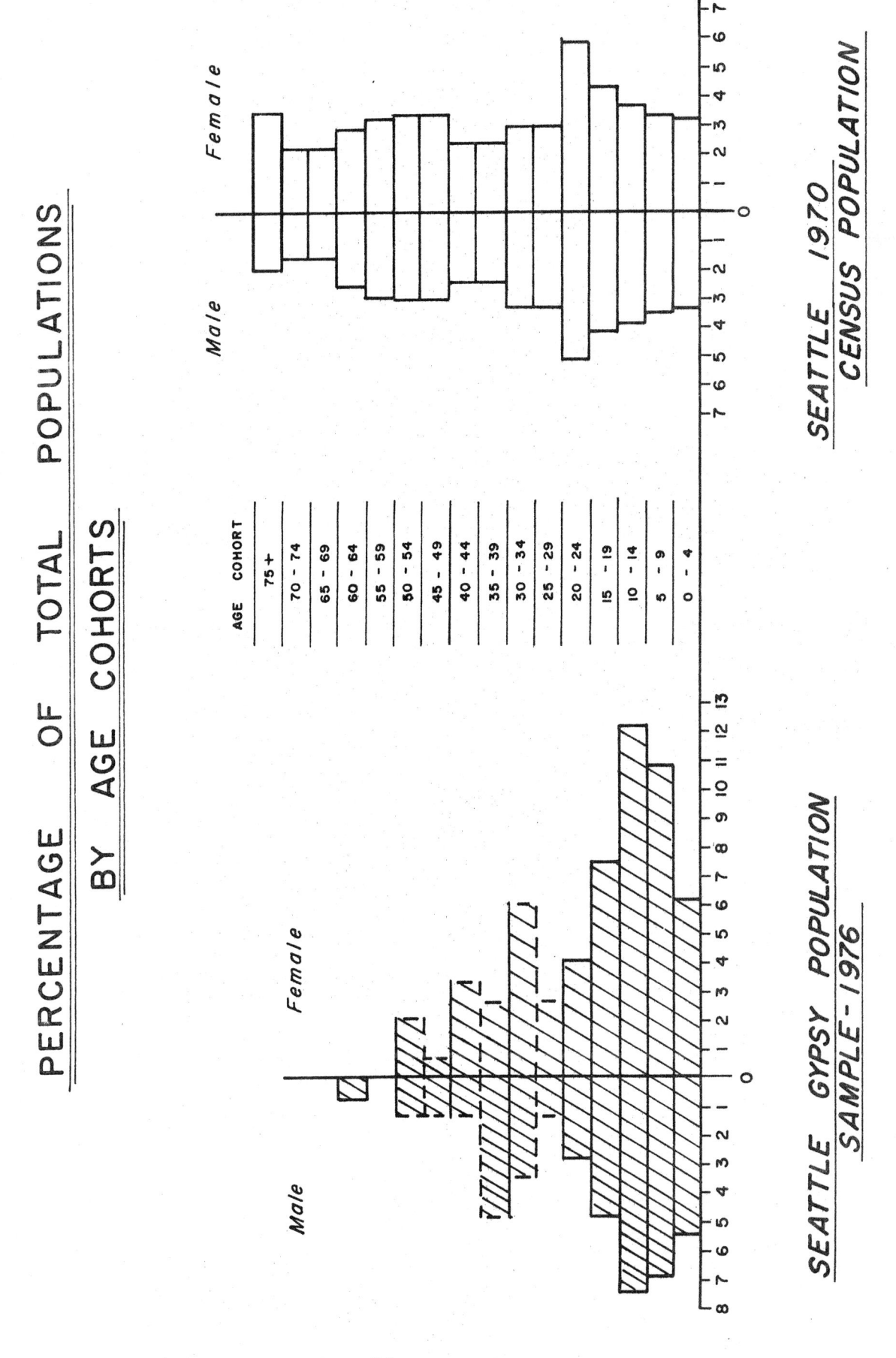

PERCENTAGE OF TOTAL POPULATIONS BY AGE COHORTS

AGE COHORT
75 +
70 – 74
65 – 69
60 – 64
55 – 59
50 – 54
45 – 49
40 – 44
35 – 39
30 – 34
25 – 29
20 – 24
15 – 19
10 – 14
5 – 9
0 – 4

SEATTLE 1970 CENSUS POPULATION

SEATTLE GYPSY POPULATION SAMPLE - 1976

relatively normal for an area with advanced technological development and a declining birth rate. It contains large percentages in the upper ages because of lowering death rates, and in part because of in-migration. There are smaller numbers in the middle years (35-45), the most economically productive years, which may be due to out-migration as well as other phenomena, including the decline in the birth rate during the war years. This was followed by the baby boom of the 1950's shown by larger numbers in the 25-35 year cohort.

In contrast the pyramid for the Gypsy population more closely resembles that of an underdeveloped country. The majority of the population (61.2%) is under the age of twenty (compared to 29.4% for Seattle) which indicates the likelihood of a high birth rate and increasing population size as the younger children enter the childbearing ages. Only 0.7% of the sample Gypsy population is over 65 years, while 13.1% of the Seattle population have reached this mature age. The national average is about 10% over 65. Excluding migration this low percentage for Gypsies could indicate a high death rate for these ages. The composition of the population shows tendencies toward high birth rates in the Gypsy population. This finding is consistent with other Gypsy populations. The early maturation and lengthened childbearing years probably causes many female Gypsies to die at a relatively young age. There may, of course, be genetic reasons for the high mortality of both male and female Gypsies but more likely poor health care, inadequate diet, and neglect of chronic conditions contribute most to the high death rate.

At present 45.3% of the women in the Seattle Gypsy population are in the childbearing 15 to 44 age group. [It has been reported that Gypsies in Seattle, as in other areas, are often mothers at ages 13 or 14 (Cemeno, 1975).] The Seattle Gadjo population on the other hand, has 40.1% of the women in childbearing ages. A more realistic indication of future birth potential is found by calculating the percentage for women now alive from age 0 to 39 years. In doing so we eliminate the women in the upper cohort, 40-44, and add the women 0 to 14 who will soon be in their productive years. The totals reveal 89.5% of all Gypsy women and 55.7% of all Seattle women will be in the childbearing years within the next 20 years. Given the assumed higher birth rate for Gypsies (Sutherland, p. 53), the extended period of childbearing years, and increasing survival rates, it is probable that there will be a substantial increase in the Gypsy population in the near future, while there will be a decrease in the number of births for the total Seattle population.

The low number of Gypsies in the aged 20 to 30 group in the sample, especially females, is likely the result of marriages into other Gypsy groups, as well as the increased amount of traveling done by households in this age group, and some out-migration.

One of the most significant differences in the two populations is the number of females. "Sex ratios at different ages follow a rather typical pattern. Normally young boys are more numerous than girls, because male births are slightly more frequent than female births. Males suffer higher death rates, with the result that they generally fall short of the number of females at higher ages" (Barclay, p. 23). The sex ratio for each of the two populations is listed by age cohort in Table 6. The Seattle Gadjo population follows the typical sex ratio pattern while the Gypsy population shows a marked excess of females in all cohorts except for those between the ages of 35-39 and 45-49. (The 60-64 cohort has only one male and no females.)

TABLE 6

SEX RATIO* FOR THE SEATTLE GYPSY POPULATION
COMPARED WITH THE SEATTLE POPULATION
(May, 1976)

Cohort	Gypsy[1]	Seattle[2]
0-4	88.9	105.3
5-9	62.5	103.8
10-14	61.1	103.4
15-19	63.6	93.5
20-24	66.7	85.0
25-29	50.0	111.7
30-34	55.6	111.7
35-39	175.0	98.2
40-44	40.0	98.2
45-49	200.0	90.3
50-54	66.7	90.3
55-59	0	90.9
60-64	100.0	88.7
65-69	0	71.7
70-74	0	71.7
75+	0	57.4
Ratio for total population	70.9	92.0

*Sex Ratio = ratio of males to females or males per 100 males:
$(\frac{M}{F})k$ = sex ratio (k=100)

[1] Sample taken by interview, 1976.

[2] Data from U. S. Census, 1970.

Not only are the two populations different but the degree of difference per 100 females is even more significant. For example, at ages 5 to 9 there are 3.8 more males per 100 females in the Seattle population. At the same time, there are 37.5 fewer males per 100 females in the Gypsy population. The sex ratios are shown graphically in Figure 7.

The two cohorts which show an excess of males in the Seattle Gypsy population are the result of men marrying younger women. It is common practice for men to marry more than once. Men who do marry more than once generally choose younger women. The clear difference between the sex ratios between the two populations is shown in a comparison of the total cohorts. The sex ratio for the Seattle population is 92.0 males for every 100 females. The ratio for Seattle Gypsies is 70.9 males for every 100 females. In spite of the small sample size, a test for statistical significance shows the sex ratio for ages 0 to 19 to be significantly different at the 0.05 level. In other words, we can be 95% certain that there is a real difference between the Seattle population and the Gypsy population. However, due to the small sample size and errors which may have occurred in recording, no further significance can be attached to the sex ratio data.

The household size of the 32 Gypsy families and the number of children in each household are shown in Table 7. Households in Seattle are considerably smaller than those reported in New York and California by Gropper and Sutherland, who both gave 8 as the average household size (Gropper, p. 61; Sutherland, p. 41). Most young people have little difficulty finding not only

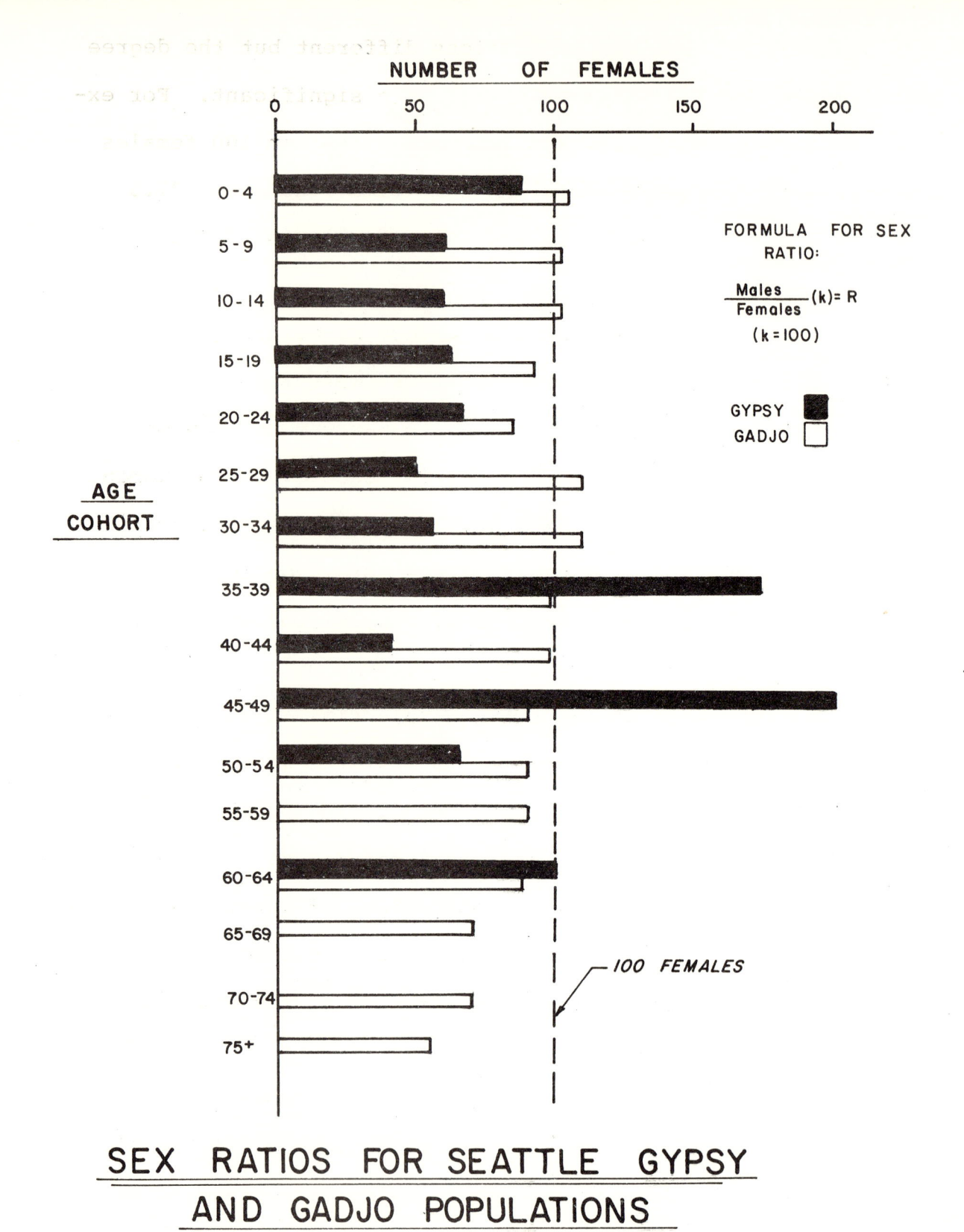

SEX RATIOS FOR SEATTLE GYPSY AND GADJO POPULATIONS

Figure 7

TABLE 7

GYPSY HOUSEHOLD SIZE AND NUMBER OF CHILDREN
IN 32 FAMILY SAMPLE

Household	Family Size	No. of children under 14
1	7	5
2	7	5
3	6	3
4	6	4
5	6	4
6	4	2
7	7	5
8	8	7
9	7	5
10	2	0
11	3	1
12	3	1
13	6	5
14	4	3
15	5	3
16	5	3
17	7	6
18	2	0
19	3	1
20	6	4
21	6	4
22	6	4
23	4	2
24	5	3
25	2	0
26	4	2
27	2	1
28	2	1
29	7	5
30	4	2
31	2	0
32	7	5

Family Size:
  Mean: 4.84
  Median: 5.0
  Mode: 6/7

Number of Children:
  Mean: 3.31
  Median: 4.0
  Mode: 5.0

accommodation but also income outside the extended family. Thus there are fewer cases of several generations living together. There is but one case in the sample in which a young married couple (boy 17, girl 15) live with the boy's parents. All other young couples have established separate households. This is another break from tradition but does show a higher degree of economic independence in the Seattle area. In Seattle 69% of the Gypsies in the sample over 14 years old are married.

Map 4 shows the approximate residential location of twelve Gypsy households in the north end of Seattle. Nine of the residences have been occupied by Gypsies for the past year. Map 5 shows the census tract location for the same residences and the number of Gypsy households in each of the tracts. At least five of the houses are owner-occupied by the Gypsies. The average assessed value of the owned housing is $20,013, compared to the median census tract value of $22,340. This valuation indicates another break with the norm, especially from Sutherland's data in which Gypsies in Barvale, California occupy substandard housing and rarely own their own homes.

There is no external difference between Gypsy houses and other houses in their neighborhoods. Seattle Gypsies seem to have requirements similar to other Gypsies when they search for a house. "First, they prefer houses located on the main streets . . . Second, closely related families tend to congregate in one area if they can. . . Third, they prefer to live in a house which has been occupied by a Rom family previously" (Sutherland, p. 58-60). In addition it can be observed in Seattle that Rom will relocate to be nearer an economic or social resource when possible. Evidence here is the drawing power of the Seattle Gypsy school. Most of the families with children in the Gypsy school now live within 3.5 miles of the school. This is a result

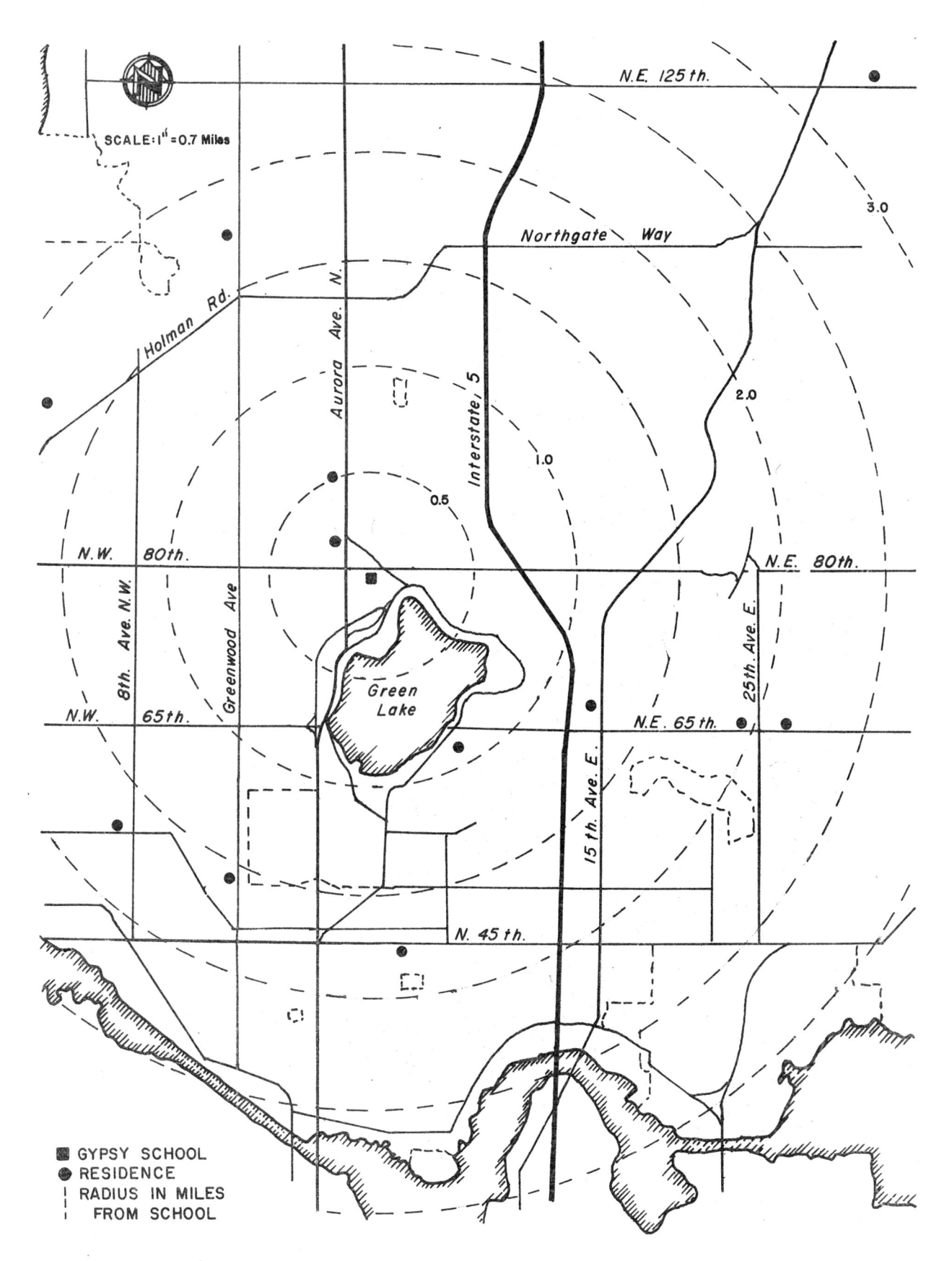

RESIDENTIAL LOCATION OF GYPSY HOUSEHOLDS IN SEATTLE, NORTHEND

MAP NO.4

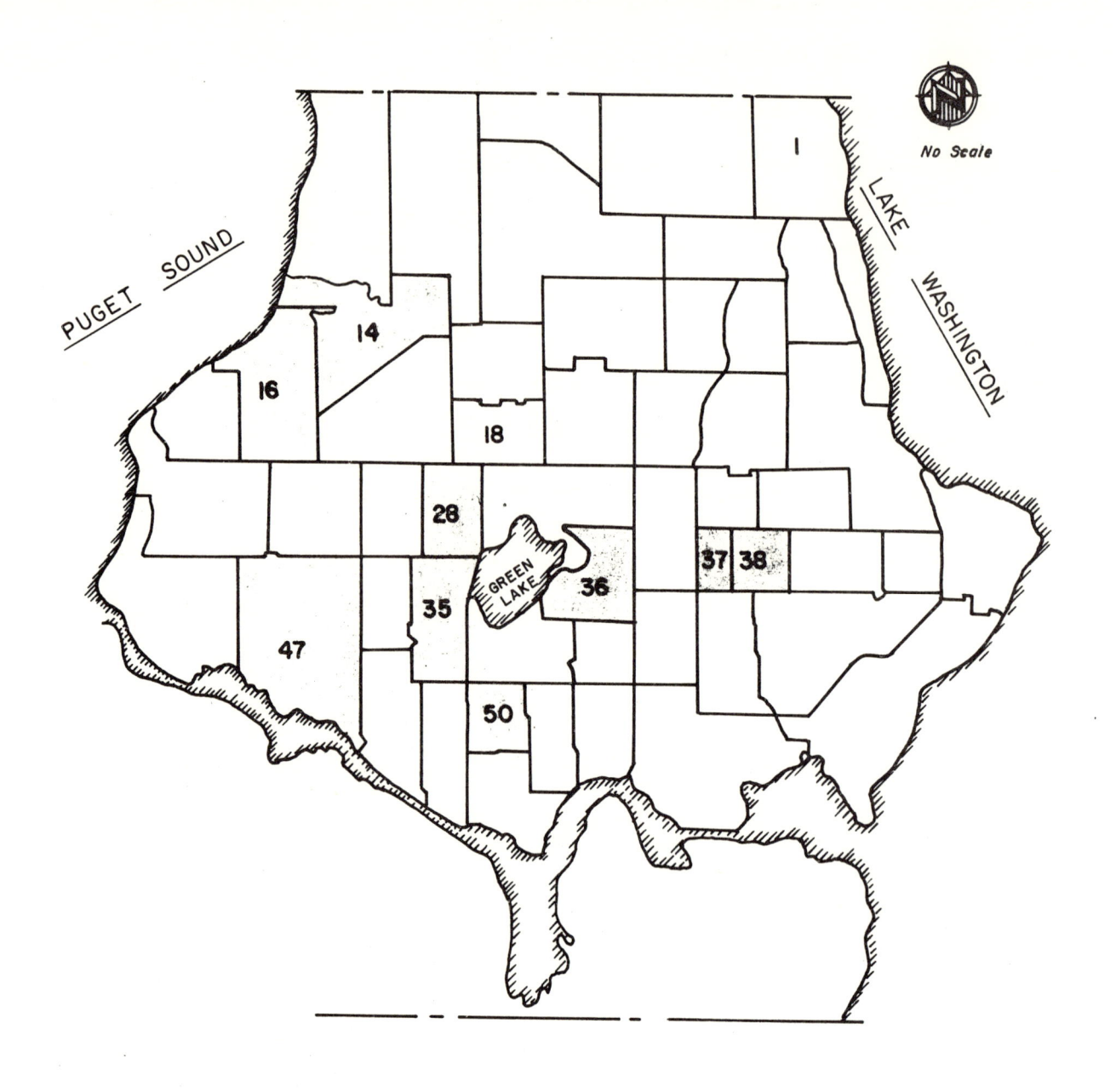

CENSUS TRACT LOCATION OF HOUSEHOLDS IN SEATTLE NORTHEND SAMPLE

MAP NO. 5

of relocation of approximately 50% of the families from other parts of the city (see Map 4).

The Gypsy Alternative School is a bilingual/bicultural program initiated by the Seattle Public Schools in the fall of 1973. The school was established in response to the requests to provide a basic educational skills and cultural adjustment to the primarily illiterate Gypsy population. The Gypsy children and their parents have traditionally avoided formal education. They often felt "academically bewildered" (URRD, 1976), have been abused by other children and are unaccustomed to being alone in an alien cultural situation. In the 1974-75 school year funding was added by the Urban, Rural, Racial and Disadvantaged Program - State of Washington (URRD) and a permanent facility at Bagley Elementary School was provided for the Gypsy Alternative School. In 1975-76 the school served 34 children with one full time teacher, one Gadjo aide and one Gypsy aide who acts as a liaison with the Gypsy community.

In the 1974-75 school year URRD provided $20,773 and the Seattle School District provided $18,884 for the Alternative School. For the 1975-76 term the figures have increased by 20% to $24,928 for URRD and $22,733 for the Seattle School District. The 1976-77 projected budget is divided between the two funding agencies as shown in Table 8.

The item of most interest is the amount allocated for pupil transportation. The money is allocated by the district and goes directly to the parents of the children. Each parent who transports his children to school is paid a fixed daily amount for each of the children he brings to class. A parent with five

TABLE 8

FISCAL BUDGET 1976-77
GYPSY ALTERNATIVE SCHOOL

		URRD	Seattle School District
1.	evaluator	$ 249	$ 0
2.	clerical	1,792	0
3.	teachers		
	head teacher	0	16,571
	two aides	21,686	0
4.	released time	254	254
5.	pupil transportation	0	4,480
6.	supplies and material	200	1,428
7.	instructional materials	347	0
8.	contractual services:		
	telephone	280	0
9.	capital outlay	120	0
		$ 24,928	$ 22,733
	TOTAL = $47,661		

SOURCE: URRD, 1976.

children attending class for five days can supplement his income with $40 to $45 per week. In addition, the children are provided with a free lunch in the Bagley school cafeteria through the Federal School Lunch Program. These immediate rewards furnish the incentive for locating near the school to cut transportation costs and thus the added benefit of locating in the proximity of other Gypsy families.

The ultimate goal for URRD and the Seattle School District is not really any different from programs in other parts of the United States or for that matter in other countries. The recurring desire is to remove Gypsies from the welfare rolls and assimilate them into the system. We should not lose sight of this fact no matter how philanthropic the stated objectives may seem.

In the proposal for funding of the school for the next term (1976-77) several objectives are set forth. They include reading achievement, attendance and basic knowledge of Gypsy history. In addition, some activities are being planned to involve interaction between Gypsy and Gadjo students at Bagley school. At present the Gypsy children are almost completely segregated from the Bagley children. Both groups use some of the same facilities (i.e. library, cafeteria, playground and restrooms) but in each of these places and the classrooms there is no mixing of the groups. The Gypsy school is in a "portable" building alongside the main school building, separate and co-existing.

More important for the Gypsy community as a whole will be innoculations from common communicable diseases, dental screening and home care instruction, plus sight and hearing examination for all students, to be made available next year.

The Gypsy Alternative School has become much more than a place for academic pursuits by students. It has evolved into a social and cultural center for varying activities in which not only students but parents as well find a link with the alien culture in which they see alternative methods for common activities.

Each year some of the URRD funds are earmarked for an evaluation by Independent URRD Auditors (IUA). A total of 63 URRD programs in the State of Washington are evaluated and compositely ranked according to their accomplishment of objectives and potential for fulfilling a specific need. The evaluation affects future funding. In this composite ranking the Gypsy Alternative

School was ranked first in the state, assuring the school of funding for the coming year (Seattle Public School Memorandum, May 7, 1976).

The Gypsy school is the major difference between Seattle Rom and other groups of Rom in the United States. There have been other schools exclusively for Gypsies, notably in San Francisco, Spokane, and some eastern cities, but they have been short lived. None of the other schools have had the success and cooperation achieved in Seattle. There is still much conjecture regarding the reasons for the success here. It could be part of the con game to get money, or perhaps just a place to send the children during the day, but there are those who believe that the Gypsy people want to get a good education and increase their employment opportunities (*Wall Street Journal*, April 14, 1975). Yet, the major strength of the program, the trust and rapport between the teacher and the Gypsy community, is also considered to be the major weakness. The communication between the teacher and the Rom could not be transferred to another Gadjo. It has taken the teacher two and a half years to achieve acceptance by the Romani community. It is to say the least, a very precarious link that holds the two together.

Gypsies in Seattle are subject to many constraints, both internal and external. Illiteracy coupled with their reliance on a limited information field, which even though sufficient for most of their needs, falls short in providing the Rom with information which would help them to operate more efficiently in Gadjo society. The Romani cultural bias contains elements which hinder integration with Gadjo; elements such as male dominance, social isolation, and independent political organization. These internal constraints are no less important than the external environmental constraints of the alien culture. The Rom are dependent on the economic stability of the Seattle area, and consequently their income is affected by changes in the surrounding area. Their school is at the mercy of the funding agencies. Yet, the Rom in Seattle, in spite of their lower income status, seem to be in much better condition than their counterparts in other areas of the country for which there has been documentation (Gropper, Sutherland, Cohn, Maas).

Social characteristics of the Seattle Gypsy population differ considerably from their Gadjo neighbors. The population is young, mobile and in a stage of population growth. Most are married and have families. In addition, the Rom are subjected to equally strong cultural stimulation. In the course of their life cycle there should be a balance in the requirements for social and cultural responsibilities in order for the individual to function within the society. Some of the demands upon individuals, and on the group as a whole, are listed below with a brief description of their requirements.

A. <u>Cultural Demands</u>

1. Maintenance of territory - the area claimed by the group must be preserved through communication with other vitsa members and by the protection of income sources.

2. Affiliation in time of stress - information regarding specialists such as doctors, hospitals, attorneys, etc. is passed through the same channels which inform

family and friends of a crisis for which they must give their support (i.e. hospital visits, trouble with Gadjo, economic crisis, etc.).

3. Arrangement of marriages - this involves communication between vitsa members, travel to locate partners and to make arrangements for bride price and the ceremony.

4. Political stability - leadership, court trials and disputes must be kept separate from Gadjo institutions, and political independence must be maintained when possible.

5. Attendance at special events - yearly festivals and feasts are held at specific times to exchange information and reinforce social commitments.

B. Social Demands

1. Maintenance of separation from the Gadjo - all social activities exclude Gadjo, and interactions must be limited to the most impersonal levels.

2. Conformance to group activities - most activities must be done in the presence of other family members or friends to offer protection and support.

3. Preservation of the extended family - women are expected to produce children in order to be accepted into the husband's family. Men want to have many children--boys, who will stay with the family and supply income and girls, who will bring income, including bride-price.

C. Economic Demands

1. Participation at all age levels - it is mandatory that everyone aid the family by bringing income. Small children are taught to assert themselves in all situations which might prove lucrative.

2. Use of limited income sources - any income source may be utilized but knowledge of new sources is limited; thus sources have become self-perpetuating-- each generation following the methods used by elders.

3. Preservation of lifestyle - includes manipulation of Gadjo, appearance of wealth, behavioral expressions (i.e. aggressiveness, coercion, etc.), maintenance of mobility and concentration on the present rather than on the future.

D. Special Consumer Demands

1. Specific housing criteria - Gypsies often require large houses to accommodate the family and frequent visitors. They have locational preferences and cost limitations.

2. Specific food requirements - young, uneducated population with heavy reliance on unnutritious, high carbohydrate foods, especially take-out convenience foods.

3. Special consumer products - includes toys, children's clothing, inexpensive everyday clothes and an abundance of evening wear. No need for products used by upper age levels. (Philosophy does not include build-

ing a standard of quality for retirement years.)
4. Utilization of special services - limited health care and preventive medicine lead to postponement of treatment until a specialist is the only alternative; use of attorneys and government agencies when needed.

All of these demands involve process, or a continuing development through change over time. Spatial expressions of these socialization processes among Seattle Gypsies show the importance of the four elements discussed in Chapter IV; territoriality, communication, mobility and consumership. These four elements, and others, are all part of the processes which produce vitsa interactions, residential sites for vitsa members, location of patronized businesses, sites for social activities, location of income sources and segregation from Gadjo.

The inherent dynamics of social activities inevitably produce spatial consequences, not only in the Gypsy population but in all populations. The Rom, by virtue of their social composition and cultural adherence, help us to more clearly see the actual process which results in a spatial exhibition.

CHAPTER 6

CONCLUSION

The object of the thesis was to examine the relationship between social processes and spatial behavior among urban Gypsies. In order to understand the complex set of behaviors exhibited in the urban environment an attempt was made to identify the underlying causes which initiate the activities. The Gypsies are a group with a distinct subculture and maintain autonomous social, political, and cultural institutions. The uniqueness of their lifestyle, and the almost complete social isolation from the host society, make them an exciting example of urban diversity.

The fact that Gypsy society exists in America relatively unnoticed by the majority of the population suggests the anonymity that can be achieved in urban life. Yet, at the same time, the Gypsies themselves have a very strong sense of community although they are without an exclusive spatial community. The strength of their social institutions bind them into cohesive units without permanent proximity to one another. All primary functions are performed within the self-sufficient cultural framework of Gypsy society.

Throughout history the Gypsy people have been faced with the fact that they were considered foreigners. They did not fit the cultural mold of the countries in which they lived and traveled. They responded to this environmental stimulus by turning inward for the emotional reinforcement necessary for their survival. The original drive toward self preservation has evolved a contemporary Gypsy society which exhibits avoidance and non-conforming behavior towards the host society.

Centuries of a nomadic lifestyle and resistance to strange Gadjo cultures have left their impact on today's Rom. Pride in being a Gypsy and preserving their way of life are of foremost importance. Resistance to being assimilated into the larger society is achieved by adaptation on one hand and flee response on the other. The Gypsies have perfected a way to manipulate the culture contact situation. Not only are they culture carriers (i.e. transporting cultural beliefs and customs from one host society to another), but they are also culture brokers, using to advantage what they have learned in other cultures. Superficial adaptation to alien cultures has protected their own lifestyle from the outside world.

The incorporation of beliefs and taboos regarding Gadjo into the cultural framework insures the perpetuation of the ethnic identity of the Rom. Young Gypsies are taught expected behaviors toward Gadjo, and are then given little opportunity for interaction with the Gadjo on a personal level.

Since leaving India, and perhaps even before then, spatial mobility has been a part of the daily existence for the Gypsies. Important symbolism is still attached to the ability to relocate at will, both residentially and for pleasure. Many of the behaviors which Gypsies display can be analyzed by the spatial patterns they produce. Propensity to move, communication, consumership and territorial preference are all evidence of social processes occurring within the Gypsy community.

It would be an error to assume that all Gypsies are alike. They have many characteristics in common as a group, but as individuals they do not completely fit the image that has been conveyed. Not only are individuals different from one another, but also groups of Gypsies in different locations have a complex set of environmental constraints to which they must adapt. The result is a wide range of behaviors, income sources and adaptations which are not exactly the same in any two places. Nevertheless, for Gypsies there are many similarities between groups that make them different from the Gadjo.

Seattle Gypsies as a group show many of the characteristics common to other Gypsy groups. They are distinguishable as a subpopulation whose activities and ethnic background differentiate them as Gypsies. Their social isolation, network of communication and daily activities separate them from the Gadjo in all ways except economic subsistence.

The fast-paced impersonal atmosphere of the urban environment afford Gypsies the opportunity to be spatially integrated in the middle class neighborhoods, while remaining socially separated from their Gadjo neighbors. The adaptation of the American Gypsy to urban areas has in great part helped them to survive. Communication and movement serves the same purpose now as did continuous propinquity in the past. The community can exist without the spatial nearness usually required to maintain group solidarity.

Study of groups like the Gypsies indicates the desirability

of understanding the hidden social processes which produce spatial behaviors and activities. The Gypsies are indeed an unusual group, but they help us to see even more clearly how society, culture and space interact in our contemporary urban environment.

BIBLIOGRAPHY

<u>Books</u>

Argyle, Michael (ed.), *Social Encounters*. Oxford: Aldine Publishing Co., 1973.

Arnstberg, Karl-Olov, *Zigenarens Väg*. Helsingborn: A. B. Boktryck, 1974.

Barclay, George W., *Techniques of Population Analysis*. New York: John Wiley & Sons, Inc., 1958.

Bee, Robert L., *Patterns and Processes*. New York: The Free Press, 1974.

Bercovici, Konrad, *The Story of the Gypsies*. New York: Cosmopolitan Book Corporation, 1928.

Brown, Irving, *Gypsy Fires in America*. New York: Kennikat Press, 1972.

Clébert, Jean-Paul, *The Gypsies*. Middlesex, England: Penguin Books, Ltd., reprinted 1970.

Cohn, Werner, *The Gypsies*. Reading, Mass.: Addison-Wesley Publishing Co., 1973.

Cotten, Rena Maxine, *The Fork in the Road: A Study of Acculturation Among the American Kalderas Gypsies*, Ph.D. Dissertation, Columbia University, 1950.

Eisenberg, J. F. and Dillon, W. S. (eds.), *Man and Beast: Comparative Social Behavior*. Washington: Smithsonian Institute Press, 1971.

Esty, Katharine, *The Gypsies, Wanders in Time*. New York: Meredith Press, 1969.

Glazer, Nathan & Moynihan, Daniel P., *Beyond the Melting Pot*. Cambridge: The MIT Press, 1970, 2nd ed.

Gordon, Milton M., *Assimilation in American Life*. New York: Oxford University Press, 1964.

Gropper, Rena C., *Gypsies in the City*. Princeton: The Darwin Press, 1975.

Hall, Edward T., *The Silent Language*. Garden City: Doubleday & Co., Inc., 1959.

————, *The Hidden Dimension*. Garden City: Doubleday & Co., Inc., 1969.

Harrington, Michael, *The Other America: Poverty in the United States*. Baltimore: Penguin Books, Inc., 1971.

Herskovits, Melville J., *Acculturation: The Study of Culture Contact*. Gloucester, Mass.: Peter Smith, 1958.

Heymowski, Adam, *Swedish <<Travellers>> and their Ancestry. A Social Isolate or an Ethnic Minority?* Uppsala: Almqvist & Wiksells, 1969.

Hinde, R. A., *Biological Bases of Human Social Behaviour*. New York: McGraw-Hill Book Co., 1974.

Ittelson, Rivlin and Proshansky, Winkel, *An Introduction to Environmental Psychology*. New York: Holt, Rinehard & Winston, Inc., 1974.

Kariel & Kariel, *Explorations in Social Geography*. Reading, Mass.: Addison-Wesley Publishing Co., 1972.

Kenrick, Donald and Puxon, Grattan, *The Destiny of Europe's Gypsies*. New York: Basic Books, Inc., 1972.

Kosinski, Leszek, *The Population of Europe*. London: Longman Geographic Paperback, 1970.

Krames, Lester; Pliner, Patricia & Alloway, Thomas (eds.), *Nonverbal Communication*. New York: Plenum Press, 1973.

Liegeois, Jean-Pierre, *Les Tsiganes*. Paris: Editions due Sevil, 1971.

McDowell, Bart, *Gypsies, Wanderers of the World*. Washington, D. C.: National Geographic Society, 1970.

McGinnies, Elliott and Ferster, C. B., *The Reinforcement of Social Behavior*. Boston: Houghton Mifflin Co., 1971.

Miller, Carol, *Macuaya Gypsy Marimé*. Master's thesis, University of Washington, 1968.

Park, Robert E., *Race and Culture*. Glencoe, Ill.: Free Press, 1950.

Phillips, D. V. McGrigor, *Catalogue of The Romany Collection*. Edinburgh: Thomas Nelson & Sons, Ltd., 1962.

Pickett, David Wayne, *Prolegomena to the Study of the Gypsies of Mexico*. These delicence, Syracuse University, 1962.

Puxon, Grattan, *Rom: Europe's Gypsies*. London: Minority Rights Group, 1973.

Quintana, Bertha B. and Floyd, Lois Gray, *¡Qué Gitano! Gypsies of Southern Spain*. New York: Holt, Rinehart & Winston, Inc., 1972.

Sanford, Jeremy, *Gypsies*. London: Secker & Warburg, 1973.

Smith, David M., *The Geography of Social Well-Being in the United States*. New York: McGraw-Hill, 1973.

Sommer, Robert, *Personal Space: The Behavioral Basis of Design*. Englewood Cliffs: Prentice Hall, Inc., 1969.

Sutherland, Anne, *Gypsies: The Hidden Americans*. London: Tavistock Publications, 1975.

Trigg, Elwood B., *Gypsy Demons and Divinities*. Secaucus, N. J.: Citadel Press, 1973.

Wedeck, H. E., *Dictionary of Gypsy Life and Lore*. New York: Philosophical Library, 1973.

Wood, Manfri Frederick, *In the Life of a Romany Gypsy*. London: Routledge & Kegan, 1973.

Yoors, Jan, *Crossing*. New York: Simon & Schuster, 1971.

_____, *The Gypsies*. New York: Simon & Schuster, 1967.

_____, *The Gypsies of Spain*. New York: Macmillan Publishing Co., Inc., 1974.

Webb, G.E.C., *Gypsies: The Secret People*. London: Herbert Jenkins, 1960.

Zelinsky, Wilbur, *The Cultural Geography of the United States*. Englewood Cliffs: Prentice-Hall, Inc., 1973.

Articles

Anderson, Gwen & Bridget Tighe, "Gypsy Culture and Health Care," 1973 (Feb.), *American Journal of Nursing*, 73(2):282-85.

Brown, Lawrence A. and Moore, Eric G., "The Intra-Urban Migration Process: A Perspective," *Geografiska Annaler*, Series B. Vol. 52, 1970. 1-13.

Clark, Marie Wynne, "Vanishing Vagabonds: The American Gypsies," *Texas Quarterly*, 10:204-10, Summer 1967.

Eibl-Ebesfelt, Irenaeus, "Transcultural Patterns of Ritualized Contact Behavior," *Behavior and Environment: The Use of Space by Animals and Men*, New York, 1971. 238-246.

<<Etudes Tsiganes>>, *Bulletin De L'Association Des Etudes Tsiganes*, Paris, issues 20e Année, No. 4, December 1974; 17e Anée, No. 4, December 1971; 19e Année, No. 3, September 1973; 18e Année, No. 2 et 3, September 1972.

Fowler, Gary & Davies, C. S., "The Urban Settlement Patterns of Disadvantaged Migrants," *Journal of Geography*, 71(5):275-284. 1972.

Golant, Stephen M., "Adjustment Process in a System: A Behavioral Model of Human Movement," *Geographical Analysis*, 3(3): 203-220. July 1971.

Goodey, Brian, "Characteristics of the English Gypsy Population," *Geographical Review*, 58:487-9. 1968.

Gropper, Rena C., "Urban Nomads--The Gypsies of New York City," *Transactions of the New York Academy of Sciences*, 29(8): 1050-56.

Hancock, Ian F., "Gypsies in Texas," *Roma*, June 1974. Vol. I Roma Publications, Chandigarh, India.

Kornblum, William & Paul Lichter, "Urban Gypsies and the Culture of Poverty," *Urban Life and Culture*, 1(3):239-253. October 1972.

Lee, Ronald, "Learn Romani," *Roma*, 1:58. June 1974.

Lowry, Mark, "Racial Segregation: A Geographical Adaptation and Analysis," *Journal of Geography*, 71(1):28-40. January 1972.

Marcinkiewicz, Stanislaw, "Bandania Mad Dermatoglifami Palców Rak Cyganów" [Studies on finger dermatoglyphics in Polish Gypsies], *Materialy I Prace Antropologiczne*, 83:309-334. (In Polish)

Miller, Carol, "Sedentary Adaptations of the Nomadic Roma Gypsies," unpublished essay submitted for publication in forthcoming book *Tinkers and Gypsies*, Rehfisch (ed.), University of Hull, England.

Okely, Judith, "Gypsy Women. Models in Conflict," pp. 55-86 in *Perceiving Women*, Shirley Ardener. New York: John Wiley & Co., 1975.

Redfield, Robert, "The Folk Society," *The American Journal of Sociology*, Vol. LII, January 1947; *Bobbs-Merrill Reprint* No. 229.

Rex-kiss, B.; Szabó, L.; Szabó, S.; and Hartmann, Eva, "ABO, MN RH Blood Groups, HP Types and HP Level GM (1) Factor Investigation on the Gypsy Population of Hungary," *Human Biology*, 45(1):41-61, 1973.

Roseman, C. L., "Migration as a Spatial and Temporal Process," *Annals*, Association of American Geographers, Vol. 61, 1971, 589-98.

Ruston, Gerard, "Analysis of Spatial Behavior by Revealed Space Preference," *Annals*, Association of American Geographers, 59(2):391. June 1969.

Seattle Times: December 4, 1962, p. 55; August 4, 1963, p. 13; July 17, 1964, p. 27; May 9, 1966, p. 9; March 26, 1968, p. 2; April 18, 1968, p. 44; March 25, 1970, p. C-11; July 21, 1970, p. B-2.

Sibley, David, "Locational Policies for Gypsies," a report on the Centre for Environmental Studies Conference, London, October 3, 1975.

Sopher, David E., "Place and Location: Notes on the Spatial Patterning of Culture," *The Idea of Culture in the Social Sciences*, Louis Schneider (ed.), Cambridge University Press, London, 1973.

Spicer, Edward H., "Persistance Cultural Systems," *Science*, Vol. 174, November 19, 1971.

SSRC Summer Seminar on Acculturation, "Acculturation: An Exploratory Formulation," *American Anthropologist* 56:973-1002. 1954.

Tokarev, S. A., "N. N. Tseboksarova," Narodi Zarobezhno, Eurodi, Vol. I, Mosuva, 1964.

Videbeck, Richard, "Self-Conception and the Reactions of Others," *Sociometry*, 23:351-9. 1960.

Wedgwood, Camilla H., "The Nature and Functions of Secret Societies," *Oceania*, Vol. I. July 1930. *Bobbs-Merrill Reprint* S-323.

Wilhelm, Hónor L., p. 156 in *The Coast*, November 1903.

Wolpert, Julian, "Migration as an Adjustment to Environmental Stress," *Journal of Social Issues*, 22:92-102.

Documents

Senate Documents, 61st Congress, 3rd Session, December 5, 1910- March 4, 1911, Vol. 9. Reports of the Immigration Commission,

"Dictionary of Races or Peoples," presented by Mr. Dillingham, December 5, 1910.

Ministry of Housing and Local Government; Welsh Office, *Gypsies and Other Travellers*, London: Her Majesty's Stationery Office, 1967.

Interviews

Cemeno, Barbara, Teacher, Seattle Public Schools, Gypsy Alternative School. Interviews regarding contemporary Gypsies in Seattle, February 1974 through July 1976.

Cohn, Werner, Professor of Anthropology, University of British Columbia, Vancouver, Canada. Interview regarding Gypsies in Vancouver, B. C. March 15, 1975.

Shapiro, Michael, Assistant Professor, Department of Asian Languages and Literature, University of Washington. Interview regarding linguistics, March 4, 1975.

Correspondence

Dr. Thomas A. Acton, London, England
Dr. Werner Cohn, University of British Columbia, Vancouver, Canada
Ian F. Hancock, University of Texas, Austin, Texas
Grattan Puxon, Skopje, Yugoslavia
Padmashri W. R. Rish, Director, Indian Institute of Romani Studies, Chandigarh, India